**simulation** |sɪmjʊˈleɪʃən|

noun

The action or practice of simulating, with intent to deceive; false pretence, deceitful profession.

A false assumption or display, a surface resemblance or imitation, *of* something.

The technique of imitating the behavior of some situation or process (whether economic, military, or mechanical, etc.) by means of a suitably analagous situation or apparatus, esp. for the purpose of study or personnel training. Freq. *attrib.*

Oxford English Dictionary

IN THIS ISSUE

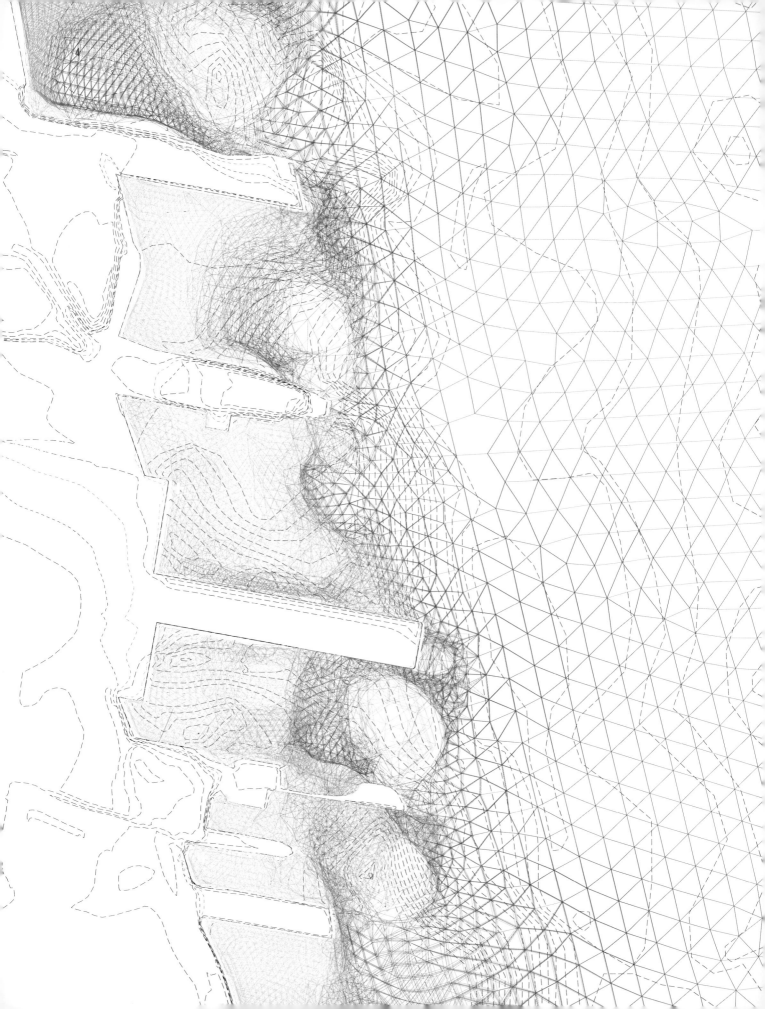

# LA+ SIMULATION
## EDITORIAL

Landscape architects are masters of simulation – our disciplinary expertise traffics in the artful practice of manipulating and mimicking nature. The degree to which landscapes should *appear* natural has long been a source of spirited debate within our discipline. Of course, disputes about the nature of simulation go far beyond landscape architecture. As a philosophical concern, simulations have been both suspected and supported as they raise questions that are at the very essence of how we come to know the world: are the mimetic properties of simulation a means to gain access to the 'real,' or are they at the root of our distance from it?

To simulate is to *feign, to pretend, or to give false appearance*; therefore, simulations carry negative connotations. If we trace an arc from Plato's cave to Baudrillard's simulacrum, simulations are defined in relation to the distinction between an original and its copy. By this definition, simulations are surface representations that mask truth and impede access to knowledge. Such interpretations see the simulated world as inherently inferior and always subordinate to the original. The other definition of simulation–as an imitation of the behavior of some situation by means of a suitably *analogous* situation– has less sinister implications. This second meaning follows Aristotelian interpretations, whereby mimesis is a fundamental creative impulse and instrument for acquiring knowledge. For instance, a simulation can be used to study a real-world 'target' at the level of its processes and behaviors–rather than its surface appearance–in order to identify correlating features between a model and the reality that it represents. Given that much of our knowledge about the physical environment is produced at a distance through various representational systems, the distinction between reality and representation is never clear-cut. LA+ SIMULATION takes this apparent gap between reality and representation as its central concern, focusing on a variety of tools and techniques that are used to understand the processes that constitute our landscapes, cities, and environments.

Simulations take many forms, both material and immaterial. Many simulations use models in order to study complex, interrelated behaviors over time. Computer simulations, in particular, have greatly expanded our knowledge in this realm. This capacity is not simply a matter of seeing the same thing in a slightly different way; rather, computer simulations reveal 'invisible' characteristics that lie beyond direct sensing or measure. In these instances, we trust our simulations to tell us things that cannot otherwise be observed, for example, the degree to which global warming can be attributed to human activities. On the other hand, the sheer quantity of data– and the power needed to process it–has in some cases led to the creation of models that are being propelled primarily by technological advances rather than by theory or empirical observation. This may be a case of the cart leading the horse instead of bringing us closer to understanding something about natural phenomena. Yet even in these instances, we may feel assured that we can always find our way back to the nature in question by subjecting our observations and conclusions to other forms of testing. But what of simulations that are not limited to representations – where there is no 'nature' to go back to? These include the making of physical entities that reproduce the function of another physical entity, such as the eventuality of digitally-printed human organs. Should these increasingly technologized natures be greeted as a matter of course? This is, after all, humanity's legacy since the invention of agriculture. Landscapes are technological by definition: we romanticize past landscapes only when their technological underpinnings have been normalized to the point of invisibility. Or should we see today's natures as altogether different? There is no doubt we have entered an era of environmental and genetic manipulation unlike any in the past.

Today's forms of simulation have given rise to exciting methodologies and access to new knowledge; they have also raised new philosophical, practical, and ethical questions. Whether simulations are digital or physical, this compelling collection of essays demonstrates that they are increasingly central to how we understand and design with nature in entirely unprecedented ways. To harness the power of simulation, landscape architects must work beyond appearances by engaging the intangible properties that comprise the complexity of nature as we understand it today. We should ask how these tools enable us to further cultivate the ecological ethos that landscape architects have long been engaged with, and to do so in ways that are meaningful to our current environmental preoccupations. Variability, uncertainty, and flux are now central to our design vocabulary and we need modes of visualization to help foster this approach as well as to convey it to others. Of course, we should not forget the importance of the other side of simulation – the seductive nature of surface and sensation. The creation of unique and powerful experiences should remain central to our craft. We, therefore, begin this issue with an essay on the essential function of fiction in the landscape imagination.

Karen M'Closkey + Keith VanDerSys
Guest Editors

GIDEON FINK SHAPIRO  SIMULATION

Gideon Fink Shapiro earned a PhD in Architecture from the University of Pennsylvania School of Design, where his dissertation traced the confluence of garden art, planning, and infrastructure in the public parks of Paris. A frequent contributor to design publications, he has collaborated on several art and design projects and taught graduate-level courses. In 2015–2016 he worked as a postdoctoral research associate at Yale's Digital Humanities Lab.

✚ HISTORY, PLANNING

Above: The 70-foot-tall Outlook Hill, part of the Governor's Island Park designed by West8, was built in part from rubble of Coast Guard housing units that once stood on the island.

Somewhere behind the modern meaning of *simulation* as a technical model for research or training purposes, there lurks the older sense of the term, which denoted a lack of integrity. "Simulation is a Pretence of what is not, and Dissimulation a Concealment of what is," the essayist Sir Richard Steele wrote in 1711.[1] Such trickery signified moral corruption.

In landscape terms, this kind of simulation would equate to some version of fake nature. Not a transparently artificial landscape, but a more insidiously deceptive counterfeit or veneer. Think greenwashing. Simulation of this sort contradicts the pursuit of ecological integrity. Moreover, it seems at odds with the logic of the other kind of simulation, the scientific or technical kind, which is supposed to produce useful knowledge and clarify what is happening beneath the surface.

But the older, more problematic use of the word actually points to something important: the disparities between surface and substance, between site and environment. Landscape and the designed environment are full of such disparities. The ground—it is no secret—comprises heterogeneous strata. How do we deal with the differences among them?

Embracing the scientific turn in landscape practice, Brian Davis and Thomas Oles recently proposed, "A landscape is not a mere surface; it cannot be defined and understood by outward appearance alone. Landscape science will fundamentally endeavor to investigate the difference between surface and substance."[2] To directly investigate and interrogate this difference no doubt constitutes a progressive

approach. But it may be only a start, at least as far as designers are concerned. As Rob Holmes observed in response, landscape architecture is "a discipline whose core depends on *making*."[3] He thus identified a third way to respond to surface–substance differences: to *make* something of them. Operating at the threshold between investigation and invention, landscape practice can selectively articulate, reframe, or embellish the disparity between tangible and intangible features.

The point is to mediate between the found, the made, and the made-up, without necessarily smoothing them over into a seamless whole. The given and the fabricated can coexist side by side under the flickering shadows of what has already passed, and what might come to pass. What we see of a landscape does not always coincide with what we know of a landscape, and still less with the impact of actions and events that could alter it for a moment, a season, or an epoch. The performance of landscape consists not just in technical operations, as David Leatherbarrow has observed, but in the unscripted or unforeseen events (climatic, human, or otherwise) that reveal its character over time.[4] To investigate the difference between surface and substance is to contemplate that which is not apparent but which, even in latent form, contributes to the identity of the site.

A hinge between the two types of simulation, the investigative and the representational, is the concept of *fiction*. Fiction suggests a scenario. As classically defined in Aristotle's *Poetics*, fiction reveals truth in the form of a *what-if*. It distills and remakes the world-as-lived into a speculative representation, something that *could be*, crafted for resonance and effect. Unlike sheer fantasy, fiction attempts to get at something real; unlike deception or falsification, it openly reveals its artifice. Landscape practice and theory operate partly in this realm of fiction, while remaining grounded in the physical realm of matter and energy. For in addition to taking account of what is observed and known, it ventures to consider the possibilities of what *could be*.

Embracing simulation as a mode of fiction helps us make sense of new tools and techniques that promise, above all, to open up new views into otherwise obscure and complex processes – in short, to clarify how landscapes work. In the first place, fiction can play an inadvertent role in investigative research simulations. Researchers attempting to model, say, erosion patterns or stormwater absorption have to select and define parameters and work within the limits of computing power. The simulated system almost inevitably reflects conscious choices and unconscious biases. As a result, the fiction of a more clear-cut and predictable world is often concealed inside even the most rigorously empirical simulation. But as analysis segues into potential intervention, positivist methodologies may also generate more overt fictions: "What happens if we change this variable or introduce this contingency?" Suddenly we are in the business of producing scenarios, perhaps even staging complete landscape dramas.

But fiction, as the realm of the *what-if*, is too potent to relegate to just a quasi-accidental byproduct of scientific method. It calls for studied cultivation and, in appropriate situations, rigorous development. Landscape fictions reflect the generative potential of the ground. They offer scenarios for occupation, action, and interpretation, while also serving as habitats with real environmental processes. Landscape fictions might disclose hidden realities or exaggerate latent tendencies. The strategic act of digging or 'un-building,' as Aaron Betsky has written, does not necessarily reveal what already exists, but rather becomes "an invention that resides in the manner of cutting or opening."[5] Fiction is especially important for connecting the findings of landscape science to the workings of the public imagination. Artists have customarily developed such fictions in the garden, reflecting a "passionate desire to construct an expression of truth through the imagination" and a creative drive that "regenerates the past by linking it to new discoveries," in the words of Michel Baridon.[6] Not only gardens and parks, but also installations, devices, stories, images, and events can render scenarios that mediate between knowledge and conjecture.

As one of the many examples of the productive use of fiction in landscape architecture today, consider the steep hills currently taking shape on the formerly flat southern tip of Governor's Island in New York Harbor, part of the new park designed by West 8.[7] Four sculpted mounds, 25 to 70 feet high, announce their own artifice by their contrast with the flat land on the northern part of the island, and by their differing programs and ecologies. Paradoxically, these entirely human-made landforms tell a story about their site. First, they are composed of rubble from demolished military buildings that formerly stood in the park. Second, they reinforce the artificial nature of this part of the island, which was created from fill in the 20th century and is now threatened by rising seas. And third, in giving visitors something they surely crave—panoramic views of the metropolis—the hills reveal the vital estuary landscape that often remains invisible but needs to be understood as part of the ground of the city.

The dual technical-fictive character of simulation can also be found in research gardens, which date back many centuries in landscape practice. Walled enclaves such as test gardens, botanical gardens, acclimation gardens, and model farms were conceived partly as simulation zones, devoted to the pursuit of useful knowledge that could, in principle, be applied to the landscapes of a whole region or nation. But the quest for instrumental knowledge was never completely separate from the quest for meaning and image. The test gardens of the past 500 years hover "between science and representation," according to Jean-Louis Fischer, who wrote that poetic and scientific content in the garden were linked together "like a symbiotic structure."[8]

Contemporary equivalents, such as the Nature Gardens at the Natural History Museum of Los Angeles County, designed by Mia Lehrer + Associates, continue to function as both science and representation. Occupying the site of a former parking lot, the 3.5-acre landscape includes a working *arroyo* (an intermittently dry stream bed), a biodiverse 'urban wilderness,' and a local pollinator garden humming with insects. The garden is a living laboratory that condenses the regional landscape into a series of ecological and cultural episodes. It serves research and pedagogical aims, but it also constitutes a grand fabrication, a scenario where visitors can rethink the landscape and their place in it.

At the other end of the spectrum lie art projects that nonetheless can reorder and reveal a landscape through acts of invention. For example, the artist Christo intends to install a temporary, three-kilometer-long floating walkway in Lake Iseo, Italy, in 2016. If all goes well, visitors will be able to feel the gentle undulations of the water beneath their feet and watch the light change as it reflects off the yellow fabric-wrapped piers, ruffled by the breeze. The project uses fiction as a speculative and ephemeral overlay, not as a replacement for the real. It amplifies sensory effects on the outer surface of the landscape. The physical shallowness of the intervention, paradoxically, has the potential to guide the visitor's attention to the combination of seen and unseen forces that constitute the lake.

Even blatantly fake natures—the artificial boulders at a zoo, or the synthetic jungle that served as the arena for battle in the first *Hunger Games* movie— can encourage viewers to interrogate superficial or static notions of landscape. Sometimes a mere name or phrase is enough to powerfully evoke an

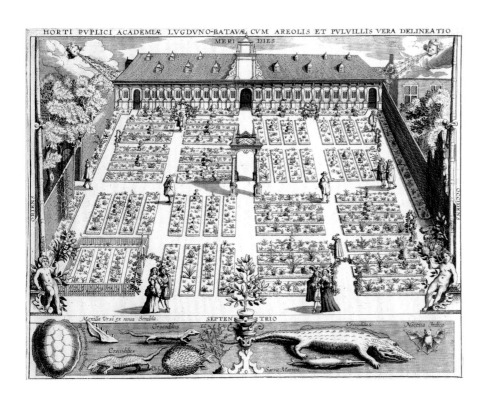

1 Richard Steele, "On Simulation and Dissimulation," *The Tatler* no. 213 (1711), quoted in *Oxford English Dictionary*.

2 Brian Davis & Thomas Oles, "From Architecture to Landscape: The Case for a New Landscape Science," *Places* (October 2014): 10.

3 Rob Holmes, "On Landscape Science," *Mammoth* (October 27, 2014), http://m.ammoth.us/blog/2014/10/on-landscape-science/.

4 David Leatherbarrow, "Architecture's Unscripted Peformance," in Branko Kolarevic & Ali Malkawi (eds), *Performative Architecture: Beyond Instrumentality* (New York: Spon/Taylor & Francis, 2005).

5 Aaron Betsky, "Dig We Must: An Argument for Revelatory Landscapes," in *Revelatory Landscapes* (San Francisco, California: San Francisco Museum of Modern Art, 2001), 13, 16.

6 Michel Baridon, *A History of the Gardens of Versailles*, trans. Adrienne Mason (Philadelphia: University of Pennsylvania, 2008), 72-73.

7 Project partners include Rogers Marvel Architects, Diller, Scofidio + Renfro, and Mathews Nielsen Landscape Architects.

8 Jean-Louis Fischer, "Introduction," *Le jardin entre science et representation: actes du 120e Congrès national des sociétés historiques et scientifiques, 1995, Aix-en-Provence* (Paris: Éditions du CTHS, 1999), 9.

unseen dimension. The slogan *Sous les pavés, la plage* (Under the pavements, the beach) rallied thousands of French students in 1968 to protest against the status quo, conjuring an alternative reality hidden just underfoot. More recently, the terms Great Pacific Garbage Patch and *gyre* have brought into focus the ominous accumulation of durable plastic litter across a huge swath of ocean. This phenomenon is difficult to observe, let alone remediate, since it sprawls across thousands of square miles and does not hold still. Most people will never directly see it. But the act of naming has provided the useful fiction of a site or a seascape, which allows people to talk about potential interventions. The descriptive metaphor of 'patch' highlights an underlying condition that otherwise remains vague and dispersed.

Landscape fiction, like investigative simulation, can help to open up places and processes that otherwise remain obscure. It therefore contrasts with simulations that merely deceive or pretend. But the aim of landscape fiction is not just to reveal underlying systems. It superimposes a scenario by digging, planting, gathering, shaping, exposing, covering, constructing, or any number of operations. Its artist-practitioners manipulate surfaces and develop the interface between what is and what could be. They must therefore be keenly interested in the differences between surface and substance. Landscape fiction demands a great deal of research and imagination plus the tact to combine them in acts of fabrication.

*Above: Engraving of the Hortus botanicus in Leiden by Willem Swanenburgh (1610).*

To do an experiment—any experiment—you need a control. A baseline state, a normal, an unmanipulated variable. A what-things-would-be-like-if-I-weren't-changing-them kind of thing. In other words, a natural thing. Then you do your experiment and see what happens, *ceteris paribus* (i.e., all other things being equal). You change a condition or two, you manipulate, you alter, and you see how your treatment cases differ from that baseline state. You determine what the interventions do and how they matter. Whether they create something better, or worse, or just different from your control. Different from that natural thing.

We are changing Earth's climate, in what the oceanographer Roger Revelle famously called humanity's "great geophysical experiment."[1] But if it's an experiment, what's the control? Changing *from what*? How is the climate we're creating different from what it *would have been* had we not dug up trillions of tons of ancient plants and animals, compressed over millions of years into soft black rock and energy-rich black goo, and sent them up in smoke, all within a couple of centuries? What would have happened instead?

To know these things, we need a control Earth. A *ceteris paribus* Earth. An Earth that would have existed had we not shown up with our hypertrophied brains, our energivorous technology, and our insatiable appetites for more and more and more. There are multiple ways to build such control Earths; the one that we'll look at here is, naturally (so to speak), climate simulation.

### Zoom: climate simulations as interscalar vehicles

A useful adage from the weather business says that climate is what we expect, whereas weather is what we get. Climate expectations are about space and time. Climate is seasons, four or two or five, depending on where you live. It's cycles of planting and harvest. It's clothing and comfort expectations tied to geography: when you'll wear short sleeves and sweat, where you'll have to bundle up in a goose-down parka and snow boots. Many terms for regions also describe climates, and vice versa: a desert, a rainforest, the tropics, the Arctic. Climates have characteristic ecosystems and iconic flora and fauna: palm trees, polar bears, camels. To a degree—pun intended—climates shape patterns of daily life: siestas on hot afternoons, huddling around fireplaces in cold winters, how and sometimes whether you can get around in rain, mud, snow, or jungle heat. For architects, climates affect buildings' structures and systems: heating and cooling, the potential for natural light, roof shapes and overhangs, load-bearing capacity, foundations, entryways, appropriate materials.

For climate control Earths, scale is the ultimate problem. In human terms, climate means patterns; stable, more or less predictable cycles; baseline states you can count on. If you live in a temperate zone, you might get some cool days next summer, but you'll be really surprised if it snows. You may travel in search of a particular climate—beach weather, dry and mosquito-free desert camping, hot days and cool evenings in the south of France—or to escape one you don't like, just as Canadian snowbirds flock to Florida each winter. In human terms, these patterns are places. They're where you live, or where you spend certain kinds of time. On the scales of ordinary human life, there's no such thing as a global climate. Rather, there are multiple climates: local and regional patterns and differences.

Yet from a God's-eye perspective (or that of a scientist) all those patterns are connected in one gigantic system, driven by colossal forces: gravity, the sun, orbital variations, axial tilt. They are shaped by atmospheric chemistry that's evolved over eons and has been altered dramatically by living things. As James Lovelock once put it, the atmosphere is the circulatory system of the biosphere.[2]

Paul N. Edwards is Professor of Information and History at the University of Michigan. He writes and teaches about the history, politics, and culture of information infrastructures. Edwards is the author of *A Vast Machine: Computer Models, Climate Data, and the Politics of Global Warming* (2010) and *The Closed World: Computers and the Politics of Discourse in Cold War America* (1996), as well as numerous articles.

＋ CLIMATOLOGY, HISTORY, INFORMATICS

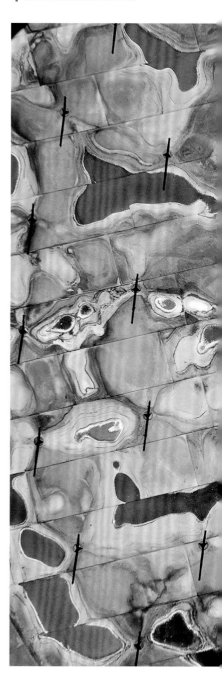

# PAUL N. EDWARDS
# CONTROL EARTH

Every year, deciduous plants suck up immense quantities of carbon in the spring when they grow leaves, and spew it out again in the fall as their fallen leaves decay, oozing carbon back into the atmosphere. Now we're adding more carbon – a lot more.

Above all, climate is driven by sun and water. Oceans absorb and release heat and carbon dioxide. Their currents, like great conveyor belts, transport heat and salt around the world. Water rises, evaporating from lakes, rivers, soil, and vegetation, only to fall again somewhere else as rain or snow. Clouds reflect solar heat back into space, trap warm air near the surface, or both. Ancient snows lie locked in mountain glaciers and in the vast ice sheets of Greenland and Antarctica. The huge fields of sea ice in the polar oceans are now shrinking, leaving polar bears, walruses, and other creatures with nowhere to rest.

Thus the spatial scales of climate physics run the gamut from the molecular (cloud nuclei, radiation-absorbing gases) to the solar system. Time scales matter just as much. Human time is measured in days, weeks, months, and years. But climate time demands perspectives of 30 years or more: decades, centuries, millennia. It's time out of mind, beyond experience, beyond human history. It's ice ages and interglacials, governed largely by solar output, orbital cycles, and the tilt of Earth's axis, with carbon dioxide as a catalyst. On the really long time scales, the positions of continents matter a lot.

Climate models make good control Earths because they can travel across some (though not all) of these scales. They're "interscalar vehicles."[3] These models are giant bundles of mathematics, expressed as computer code, that try to capture the major forces responsible for climate and examine them in interaction. The most comprehensive ones, called Earth system models (ESMs), simulate the global circulation of the atmosphere and oceans: snow and ice, with their radiative effects; clouds; land surface characteristics, such as mountains and albedo (reflectance); aerosols, both natural and anthropogenic; and the carbon cycle, including anthropogenic greenhouse gases. Carving up the atmosphere and oceans into grid cells, these simulations calculate transfers of mass, energy, and momentum from one cell to all its neighbors, on a time step of 10 minutes or so, over tens to hundreds of simulated years. Climate models are very similar to weather forecasting models, but their grid cells are bigger because a climate simulation must be run for at least several (simulated) decades. Some runs model time periods of 1,000 years or more. All this requires tremendous computer power.

Climate models can be operated like zoom lenses. For a spatial zoom, they can bring a particular region into sharper focus by embedding higher-resolution regional models into the main model. Or their results can be downscaled

using statistical methods (though this technique remains problematic and controversial). For a temporal zoom, their parameters can be set to resemble those of some previous time period. You can recreate the Pangaea supercontinent of 200 million years ago, or conditions at the peak of the last ice age, or any time you like, including the future. That's where those scary curves come from, some of them showing temperatures soaring by 5°C or 6°C (i.e., 9 or 10°F) by the end of this century. What happens if we keep on adding carbon? What happens if we stop?

### *historical* vs. *historicalNat*: versions of the past

Consider the Coupled Model Intercomparison Project (CMIP), now a crucial element of the modeling work that goes into the periodic reports of the Intergovernmental Panel on Climate Change (IPCC). CMIP helps modelers to evaluate the strengths and weaknesses of their models. It organizes a set of standard experiments in order to make apples-to-apples comparisons of model results. A 'standard experiment' means a model run, or an ensemble (i.e., a related set) of runs, using predetermined parameter values for such variables as greenhouse gases, sulfate aerosols, and solar irradiance. Experiments that project future climate change get the most press, but simulations of the past provide a better basis for model comparison, since these simulations can be compared with actual observational data. As I argued in *A Vast Machine*, CMIP's experiments play a critical role in the climate knowledge infrastructure.[4]

Various climate model intercomparison projects have been running since 1989. CMIP5 provided input to the IPCC's Fifth Assessment Report (AR5), released in 2014. Here are some CMIP5 experiments:

- *piControl* (preindustrial control run): atmospheric composition and land cover fixed at values for the year 1850; it does not include volcanic eruptions.
- *historical* (also known as *20th century*): 1850–2005, including all observed changes (both natural and anthropogenic) to atmospheric composition (greenhouse gases, volcanic eruptions, and aerosols), as well as time-evolving land cover.
- *historicalNat*: 1850–2005, but including only natural changes and events such as major volcanic eruptions, introduced in the years they occurred.
- *past1000*: time-evolving conditions over the last 1,000 years, including solar variations and volcanic aerosols.
- *midHolocene*: orbital parameters and greenhouse gases set to their states halfway through the current interglacial period (the Holocene Epoch), i.e., 6,000 years ago.
- *lgm* (last glacial maximum): orbital parameters, solar output, ice sheets, and greenhouse gases set to their conditions at the height of the most recent ice age, 21,000 years ago.[5]

All climate modeling groups wishing to contribute to the Fifth Assessment Report were required to submit a core set of experiments that included *historical* and *piControl*. The *historical* run was intended to determine the models' skill in reproducing climate trends since 1850, the period for which reasonably reliable instrument observations are available. Since climate exhibits natural as well as forced variability, the goal of *historical* is *not* to reproduce exactly the year-by-year changes that occurred–indeed, if a model did so, it would immediately be rejected as illegitimate–but to capture the overall trend. Models should, however, reflect the abrupt, short-term global cooling induced by large volcanic eruptions. Meanwhile, these should not appear in *piControl* runs, which are designed to produce an idealized steady-state baseline – that is, an Earth frozen in time, without volcanic eruptions, changes in solar output, or other natural causes of climate change. The other runs described above belonged to an optional set of "Tier 1" experiments. *midHolocene* and *lgm* were intended to show that models can reproduce global climate from 6,000 and 21,000 years ago, respectively, while *past1000* covered the period since 1000 AD using time-evolving parameters.

These temporal zoom-ins help to build confidence in climate models, as well as to diagnose their biases and areas of difficulty. They also exhibit different relationships to the real Earth – or rather to our knowledge about the real Earth, which has important limits.

*historical* runs have their own, familiar kind of control Earth, namely the historical instrument records preserved from ships, weather stations, and satellites. Nothing gets closer to what 'really' happened than that. Yet as I showed in *A Vast Machine*, those data are themselves produced by certain kinds of models. The instrument record consists of many types of information, obtained by instruments with widely varying characteristics, recorded by diverse individuals and institutions under different regimes of standards and political arrangements. To assemble anything resembling a coherent global data set, you have to reconcile these differences, a process that involves considerable investigation and adjustment. I call this "making data global." So even though the instrument record will always be our most accurate and trustworthy control Earth, it is always already the result of a certain

**1** Roger Revelle & Hans E. Suess, "Carbon Dioxide Exchange between the Atmosphere and Ocean and the Question of an Increase of Atmospheric CO2 during the Past Decades," *Tellus* 9, no. 1 (1957): 18–27.

**2** Lynn Margulis & James E. Lovelock, "The Atmosphere as Circulatory System of the Biosphere: The Gaia Hypothesis," *CoEvolution Quarterly* 6 (1975): 30–41.

**3** I owe this lovely phrase to Gabrielle Hecht, "Toxic Tales from the African Anthropocene," oral presentation, Stanford University Dept. of History, April 2015.

**4** Paul N. Edwards, *A Vast Machine: Computer Models, Climate Data, and the Politics of Global Warming* (Cambridge, MA: MIT Press, 2010).

**5** K. E. Taylor, R. J. Stouffer, & G. A. Meehl, "A Summary of the CMIP5 Experiment Design," http://cmip-pcmdi.llnl.gov/cmip5/docs/Taylor_CMIP5_22Jan11_marked.pdf; Pascale Braconnot, et al., "Evaluation of Climate Models Using Palaeoclimatic Data," *Nature Climate Change* 2, no. 6 (2012): 417-24; Keith Lindsay, et al., "Preindustrial-Control and Twentieth-Century Carbon Cycle Experiments with the Earth System Model CESM1(BGC)," *Journal of Climate* 27, no. 24 (2014): 8981–9005.

**6** G. C. Hegerl & M. R. Allen, "Origins of Model-Data Discrepancies in Optimal Fingerprinting," *Journal of Climate* 15, no. 11 (2002): 1348-56; G. C. Hegerl, et al., "Detecting Greenhouse-Gas-Induced Climate Change with an Optimal Fingerprint Method," *Journal of Climate* 9, no. 10 (1996): 2281-2306; S. H. Schneider, "Detecting Climatic Change Signals: Are There Any "Fingerprints?," *Science* 263, no. 5145 (1994): 341–47.

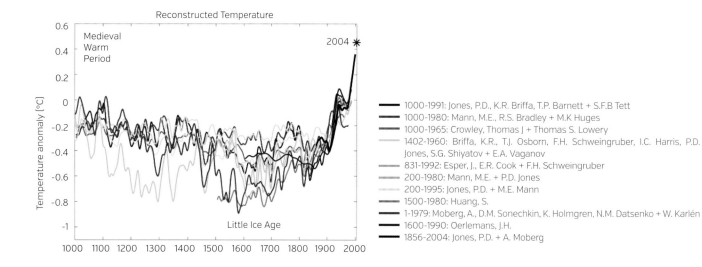

kind of modeling. This modeling accounts for the small but noticeable differences among the historical climate datasets produced by climate data centers such as the US National Climatic Data Center, the Climatic Research Unit of the University of East Anglia, and the European Centre for Medium Range Weather Forecasts.

What about *past1000, midHolocene,* and *lgm?* Here the question of the control Earth takes on a new form. On these time scales, almost all data about the real Earth's history come not from instrumental measurements but from proxies such as tree rings, ice cores, pollens, corals – things that vary with temperature or other climatic phenomena. Tiny bubbles of prehistoric air, trapped in the glaciers of Greenland and Antarctica, provide one of the few sources of directly measurable data. Moreover, for most proxies, the data come from a relatively small number of sources, unevenly distributed across the globe, and mostly on land. As demonstrated by the large differences among different proxy reconstructions, even the best data still display considerable uncertainty. When placed beside them, *past1000, midHolocene,* or *lgm* runs start to look more like control Earths in their own right (above).

But it is *historicalNat* that interests me most. These runs represent the Earth without us, or at least without the exploding populations and epic fossil fuel consumption of the 20th century. It's Earth as it might have been in the times of our great-great-grandparents, time still within historical memory, before the massive ramp-up of technology-intensive societies we built with coal, oil, and natural gas (not to mention our 1.3 billion methane-belching cattle).

*historicalNat* plays a significant role in 'attribution,' scientists' term for relating (attributing) the effects of climate change to particular causes. After all, many natural factors such as solar output and volcanic eruptions change (or 'force') the

climate. *historicalNat* helps to disentangle these natural contributions from those of human beings by giving us control Earths against which to contrast the results of our 'great geophysical experiment.'

Note the plural. *historicalNat* provides not a single control Earth but many related ones. It creates a shimmering, slightly out-of-focus vision, an ensemble of could-have-been-Earths rather than a single definitive one. The same goes for the *historical* runs: they are not exactly controls, yet still are climate histories-that-might-have-been. In climate science, the question is never "Which is the *real* control Earth?" but rather "What is the plausible range of climate on these control Earths?" If human activities don't affect the climate much, we would expect *historicalNat* to generate at least a few control Earths that look a lot like the historical instrument record.

But...we don't. The graphs on the opposite page show CMIP3 (a previous version) along with CMIP5. At both the left and the right, the yellow and gray lines show many runs from those experiments; the thick gray and red lines are the averages of the ensemble of runs, while the black line indicates the observed global temperature trend. Part (a) shows *historical* runs, while part (b) shows *historicalNat.* The inset displays three of the major global temperature records, which agree closely but not exactly, as discussed above.

Part (a) shows that although individual runs bounce around a lot (like the real climate), the ensemble of *historical* runs matches up pretty well with the observational record. In other words, as a group the climate models do pretty well at reproducing what actually happened. In general, they capture the short-term cooling caused by major volcanic eruptions and match the long-term warming trend. They're plausible simulations of history.

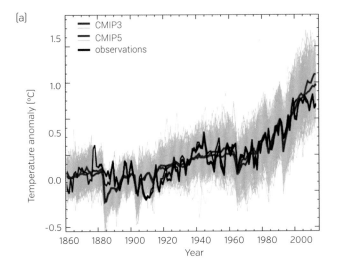

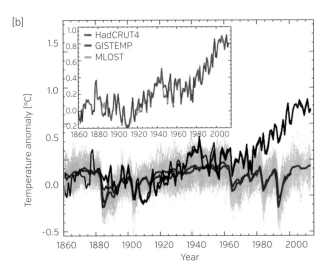

In part (b), things get really interesting. Here we're looking at control Earths without human greenhouse gases and aerosols. Part (b) tells us that until around 1960, what happened on the real Earth could also have happened on a lot of control Earth(s). But starting around 1960–exactly when fossil fuel consumption began to really spike, rising from less than two gigatons of carbon per year in 1960 to nearly 10 gigatons a year in 2010–the real Earth and the control Earths begin to diverge. From 1960 to 1980, a few control Earths still just barely match the temperature increase that occurred on the real Earth. After 1980, *none* of the control Earths even come close to reproducing the warming trend that Earth has actually experienced. In other words, without the human contributions–and not only the warming caused by anthropogenic greenhouse gases, but also the cooling caused by anthropogenic aerosols–the control Earths *would not have warmed*.

There are other simulated control Earths. Lots of them, in fact. In CMIP5, for example, there's also *historicalGHG*, a control Earth including anthropogenic greenhouse gases, but without anthropogenic aerosols. *historicalGHG* control Earths warm *more* than the real Earth has, thus showing how aerosols' cooling effect masks the underlying greenhouse trend. Among other things, simulated control Earths generate predictions of things to look for on the real Earth. Scientists call these the 'fingerprints' of particular causes: if the sun is the cause, for example, days and nights should warm equally (they don't).[6]

## Conclusion

Control Earths matter to scientists because there's no other way to tell what would have happened without us, or to disentangle the contributions of various natural and human factors. The control Earths that matter to the rest of us are the ones that involve the future. They're the 'representative concentration pathways' and emissions scenarios of the IPCC reports. These are worlds that might be, destinies that we might endure or celebrate, depending on the choices we make–or fail to make–from now on. Whatever path we actually choose will be our 'grand geophysical experiment.' Simulations give us one way, perhaps the only way, to know how much we have mattered and will matter to the planet's fate.

Above: (a): *historical* runs from CMIP3 and CMIP5 vs. observations (black line). (b): *historicalNat* runs vs. observations. Inset: global averages from instrument records, as calculated by three different climate data centers. IPCC caption: "Three observational estimates of global mean surface temperature (black lines) from Hadley Centre/Climatic Research Unit gridded surface temperature data set 4 (HadCRUT4), Goddard Institute of Space Studies Surface Temperature Analysis (GISTEMP), and Merged Land-Ocean Surface Temperature Analysis (MLOST), compared to model simulations (CMIP3 models – thin blue lines and CMIP5 models – thin yellow lines) with anthropogenic and natural forcings (a), and natural forcings only (b). Thick red and blue lines are averages across all available CMIP5 and CMIP3 simulations respectively. All simulated and observed data were masked using the HadCRUT4 coverage (as this data set has the most restricted spatial coverage), and global average anomalies are shown with respect to 1880–1919, where all data are rst calculated as anomalies relative to 1961–1990 in each grid box. Inset to (b) shows the three observational data sets distinguished by different colours." "CMIP3 and CMIP5 runs" from Gareth S. Jones, Peter A. Stott, & Nikolaos Christidis, courtesy of Paul N. Edwards, used with IPCC Permission. Adapted from Figure 10-1 of N.L Bindoff, et al., "Detection and Attribution of Climate Change: from Global to Regional," in T.F. Stocker, et al. eds., *Climate Change 2013: The Physical Science Basis. Contribution of Working Group I to the Fifth Assessment Report of the Intergovernmental Panel on Climate Change* (New York and Cambridge: Cambridge University Press, 2013), 867–952. doi:10.1017/CBO9781107415324.022.

# MICHAEL F. ALLEN
# IF YOU WANT TO UNDERSTAND NATURE,
# STICK YOUR HEA

**Michael F. Allen** is Distinguished Professor in the Departments of Plant Pathology and Microbiology, and Biology at the University of California, Riverside, where he is also Director of the Center for Conservation Biology and Chair of the Department of Biology. Allen is pioneering groundbreaking monitoring and modeling techniques of micro-scale, dynamic environmental processes that can inform larger spatial decision-making protocols; in particular, those that enable scientists to better evaluate the impacts of rising levels of carbon dioxide on natural and agricultural ecosystems.

✚ BIOLOGY, SOIL SCIENCES

In a cubic meter of soil there can be as many as 10 million organisms, comprised of thousands of species and organized into complex food webs. Even something as simple as soil respiration—the amount of carbon dioxide produced through underground processes—becomes extraordinarily complex. Respiration depends upon the particular biochemical activities of local organisms that produce local $CO_2$ concentrations. Each enzyme is slightly different, and the changes in activity are nonlinear across large temperature ranges and vary from one taxon to another. Soil structure, organic matter, and bio-physical chemistry can vary as much across an inch as between biomes.[1]

Understanding soil ecology requires observing and measuring multiple, independent variables in a spatially explicit manner over time and space. This is a critical step in managing ecosystem processes. Soils comprise the second-largest global carbon pool and the largest pool per unit of surface area on earth, with more than twice the amount of carbon as in the atmosphere.[2] However, what happens in soils does *not* stay in soils. How we measure soil carbon dynamics is critical to global carbon cycling estimates. Spatially and temporally explicit imagery and sensor data must be combined and integrated into big-data management systems to provide new linkages between human observers, camera observation systems, large-scale data acquisition and availability, and ecosystem models.

I propose a fundamental shift in integrating models and sensor-based observation systems in order to understand ecosystems and thereby simulate nature.

The development of weather forecasting provides a useful analogy. Lewis Richardson outlined the fundamental equations for predicting weather.[3] These were built on only four independent variables (time, elevation, longitude, and latitude) and seven measurable variables (wind velocity in two directions, vertical wind, air density, mass of water vapor, temperature, and pressure). Richardson divided the globe into spatial derivatives to calculate finite differences, and into time derivatives to calculate independent time steps. Using the power of the telegraph, he could collect these datasets from multiple locations, creating mosaics (or checkerboards) of the initial conditions. Using the temporal derivatives from a point, he could calculate the rates of change. His initial attempt, however, was extraordinarily wrong.

Importantly, the equations were correct. The problem lay in the frequency of measurement. The dynamics of weather involve shifts in crucial variables that occur

IF YOU WANT TO UNDERSTAND NATURE, STICK YOUR HEAD IN THE SAND!

18

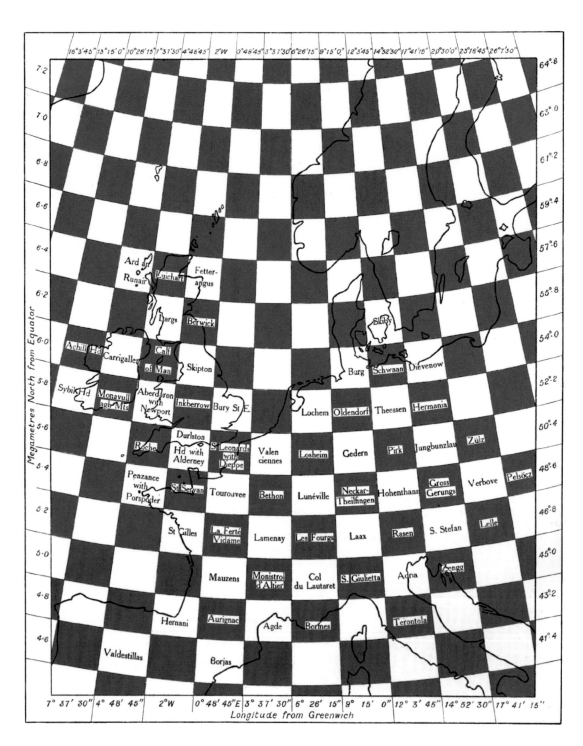

Frontispiece from Lewis F. Richardson, *Weather Prediction by Numerical Process* (Cambridge: Cambridge University Press, 1922).

at far more rapid time scales than his data inputs could capture. Specifically, Richardson averaged instantaneous pressure readings to interpolate between longer time periods; however, when immediate pressure changes create gradients, these in turn cause oscillations that result in weather dynamics. By using smoothing techniques to apply his instantaneous readings to the intervening cross time intervals, he simply missed the movements of weather fronts that regulated the downstream weather. The less frequent his measurements were, the more inaccurate his smoothing techniques, resulting in missed critical events.

I believe that this same perspective reveals the fundamental flaw in describing soil processes. Global change models increasingly suggest that events and thresholds, not gradual patterns, regulate the patterns that emerge from environmental change. To document those impacts, continuous observations and continuous measurements are absolutely essential and must be collected at the time scales in which the crucial events occur. Large-scale measurements provide patterns that emerge from driving processes such as land management practices and environmental change, but they often cannot identify the organisms, or the interactions of these organisms with each other and with the environment, that drive those processes. By contrast, soil cores, which represent points in the larger spatial unit, can often identify the driving organisms; however, the problem with core soil samples is that they are single time-point measurements that cannot be repeated. After one core sample is taken does a second core sample represent a change in time or in space compared to the first? Actually, it reflects changes in both. Two points separated in space, even though often presented as 'replicates,' can be as different in microbial composition, soil chemistry, or physical characteristics as the difference between deserts and rainforests.

Similarly, commonly used process models like DayCENT or HYDRUS are point models just like Richardson's upstream locations for weather measurements. They build on basic site information consisting of independent variables that describe site soil characteristics such as texture, and measurable, fluctuating data, including daily meteorological variables and monthly averages. These measurements are superimposed on a suite of long-term data sets to create dynamics at points. They can be taken across points to create spatial patterns thus constructing an ecosystem, or landscape-scale assessment of critical processes such as carbon cycling and sequestration. Unfortunately, these assessments essentially represent a complex ecosystem-level parallel to Richardson's weather model. The problem is the same in that measurable variables (temperature, moisture, soil organism activity) shift far more rapidly than annual, monthly, or even daily averages would reveal. Environmental events such as a freeze, atmospheric pressure change, or rainfall cause immediate shifts in $CO_2$ and $O_2$ diffusion coefficients, change biochemical activity (such as respiration or photosynthesis), and even trigger microbial and fine root mortality and growth.

## A Soil Ecosystem Observatory System (SEO)

Sensors and imaging are changing the way we measure ecosystem behavior; as the above discussion shows, we must also design interacting sensors and observation platforms that can provide high-resolution temporal data to address the 'missed event' problem. At the Center for Embedded Networked Sensing, an NSF-funded Science and Technology Center, a team of ecologists and engineers began to develop systems capable of linking mechanistic, frequent, small-scale observations and ongoing sensor data that could be integrated into larger-scale pattern descriptions of ecosystem processes. The product is known as the Terrestrial Ecology Observatory System (TEOS). We developed Rhizosystems, LLC to continue this approach. From this effort, we designed and built an in situ, automated minirhizotron (AMR) system using USB-port microscopes embedded in a motor-controlled sled that collects images inside a transparent tube in the soil. These AMR's were networked to allow for high-resolution imagery, high repeatability, and virtually continuous observation; they were also integrated with sensor data, gathered from a network of soil sensors of varying depths, measuring $CO_2$, temperature, moisture, and $O_2$. Using in situ camera systems and sensors we captured short time frames (minutes to hours or days, depending on the variable), observed how organisms behave in response to rapid change (e.g., exhibiting increased mortality or stimulated growth), and detected events that alter soil composition. In other words, by determining the balance of respiration (C) and energy (heat), we could link the actual process of carbon exchange with the AMR observations of growth and mortality.

We then needed to collect images and transform them into quantifiable data. A full tube scan usually takes approximately 34,000 images, which are organized into mosaics using RootView, a software developed by Rhizosystems, LLC (p. 21). From the images, movies can be made and roots or hyphae (branching filaments that constitute the mycelium of fungus) can be quantified using RootFly, a digitizing software that facilitates minirhizotron image analysis. More recently, we have developed image recognition software that facilitates rapid quantification in space or time of root and hyphal images. We were able to convert images to quantifiable hyphal or root length data at diurnal time scales for root and hyphal dynamics.

Our next step, currently underway, is to transform coupled image-sensor data into process-level dynamics, such as production, turnover, grazing, or predation. Among the critical steps in this effort, one specifically was to determine the appropriate spatial and temporal scales of response

for the measurable variables that equaled processes at the scale at which ecosystem dynamics occurred. To scale up to larger-scale ecosystem management or modeling, we need to interpret signals efficiently and extrapolate to spatial and temporal scales of interest.

Currently, we are measuring root and hyphal dynamics in a tropical rainforest, a mixed conifer forest, and a hot desert. Colleagues are also measuring these dynamics in a taiga bog and an alpine meadow. These measurements provide us with quantitative daily changes in biomass for multiple ecosystem types. From these daily dynamics we can see how soil organisms are behaving in response to global environmental change. Their responses will indicate if soil feedback to global change is ameliorating that change, or synergistically driving an even worse response.

Estimating $CO_2$ sinks and sources is currently undertaken at satellite-pixel-scale measurements, whether through satellite imagery or eddy covariance towers whose footprints are in the same spatial scale. Importantly, the biota represents an important sink as well as net flux for understanding global carbon balance.[4] But studying global change means scaling complex dynamics from small units to a global scale. Climate change refers to the longer-term manifestations of meteorological conditions. Thus, understanding climate change entails spatially and temporally scaling meteorological measurements to larger areas of the globe and time sets lasting decades or centuries. Today, instead of point measurements sent by telegraph as in Richardson's day, meteorologists depend upon satellite imagery, but the inherent process is the same. Defining the measurement units, though, remains difficult. As one atmospheric scientist recently noted, scaling from a satellite image pixel (on the order of 10 to 100 m2) to North America is a daunting task on the order of 11 orders of magnitude.

Just as critically, moving from biochemical processes to a single pixel is a comparable challenge, because scaling from the respiration of a single hypha to that of a pixel is an increase of approximately 14 orders of magnitude.[5] How can we proceed? We must first understand the variation in the dynamics of individual microbes and then assess how those dynamics interact and relate to ecosystem processes. We observed and measured the dynamics of individual fungi to evaluate diurnal activity and estimate total carbon allocation to mycorrhizal fungal hyphae. However, other analyses that do not include field observations of hyphal activity cannot measure turnover. All these techniques must estimate (read 'guess') microbial lifespans from laboratory incubations. From these direct field observations we can begin to build models of factors that drive root and hyphal growth, respiration, and mortality. Simple multiple regressions provide powerful tools for comparing drivers of soil organism activity. Newer path analyses also provide important clues as to drivers. Because

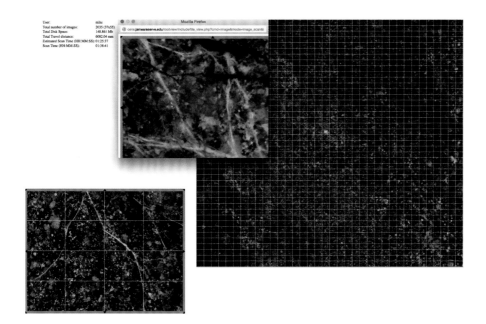

1 John N. Klironomos, Matthias C. Rillig, & Michael F. Allen, "Designing Belowground Field Experiments with the Help of Semi-Variance and Power Analyses," *Applied Soil Ecology* 12 (1999): 227-38; Michael F. Allen & James A. MacMahon, "Impact of Disturbance on Cold Desert Fungi: Comparative Microscale Dispersion Patterns," *Pedobiologia* 28 (1985): 215–24.

2 Fluxes of carbon between soil and the atmosphere, by definition, are slightly less than between vegetation and the atmosphere, but the small differences represent carbon sequestration. Sequestration is the process whereby carbon dioxide in the atmosphere was reduced from toxic to habitable concentrations over millennia.

3 Lewis F. Richardson, *Weather Prediction by Numerical Process* (Cambridge: Cambridge University Press, 1922); Peter Lynch, "The Origins of Computer Weather Prediction and Climate Modeling," *Journal of Computational Physics* 227 (2008): 3431–44.

4 Elena Shevliakova, et al. "Historical Warming Reduced Due to Enhanced Land Carbon Uptake," *Proceedings of the National Academy of Sciences* 110 (2003): 16730–35.

5 Michael F. Allen, et al. "Soil Sensor Technology: Life within a Pixel," *BioScience* 57 (2007): 859–67.

6 Rodrigo Vargas, et al. "Multiscale Analysis of Temporal Variability of Soil CO2 Production as Influenced by Weather and Vegetation," *Global Change Biology* 16 (2010): 1589–1605.

these are often nonlinear and unrelated, or distantly related, inputs (e.g., soil temperature versus depth of roots versus soil moisture), we characterize these as complex drivers of microbial processes.

Finally, we need new statistical approaches. As an example, we coupled wavelet/coherency models to study the periodicity of soil respiration and to examine repeatable temperature and moisture regimes that range from minutes (sunflecks) to seasons.[6] We are expanding beyond these simple variables into complex signal-processing approaches like coupled wavelet/coherency analyses. For example, in situ hyphal and root observations coupled with $CO_2$ measurements allow us to visualize when root or microbial activity results in $CO_2$ being respired from the soil surface, as opposed to when other chemical or physical phenomena may alter gas pathways.

Although it is important to test the parameters and outputs of models against sensor data, I believe we have reached a point where we can move beyond these datasets and into ecosystem forecasting. Instead of simply 'validating' output whenever we have a measured parameter ($CO_2$ concentrations, $H_2O$ fluxes, fungal turnover, or standing crop), the actual data from those values should be transmitted directly into the models as inputs, not outputs. Having the measured meteorological data as high temporal and spatial resolution inputs is what makes meteorological forecasting so powerful and such an important contributor to today's society. With a high level of spatial and temporal resolution and more reliable forecasting, climate studies become far more accurate and our knowledge of the impacts of anthropogenic greenhouse gas production relative to ecosystem sequestration becomes a critical tool for managing global ecosystems. With such information at our disposal, forest and agricultural ecosystems can be better managed, and we can better understand and quantify the ecosystem sequestration services of desert and shrub wildlands.

Above, top: A portion of a mosaic and an individual image (inset) from the James River Reserve, December 15, 2012. Within the inset image are roots, rhizomorphs, and fine hyphae in the matrix of soil particles.

Above, bottom: A portion of a mosaic showing 16 grid cells.

# WONDERING ABOUT WANDERING

## DANA TOMLIN

Dana Tomlin is a Professor of Landscape Architecture and City and Regional Planning at the University of Pennsylvania and an Adjunct Professor at the Yale School of Forestry and Environmental Studies, where his work focuses on the development and application of geographic information systems (GIS). Tomlin is the originator of Map Algebra, the computational language embodied in most of today's raster-based GIS software.

➕ COMPUTER SCIENCES, SPATIAL ANALYTICS

**F**igure 1 tells a story. It is a story that can be understood at a glance, a story that traces the irregular path of something that has moved through space and time. That something might be a pedestrian, a vehicle, an animal, or a storm. It could be a crime spree, an epidemic, or even a wandering eye.

In any case, this story is one from which meaningful inferences can also be drawn at a glance. Surely you can see the areas of higher concentration in that figure. If you look carefully, you might even be able to distinguish among concentrations that occur in the same locale but at different periods of time. Each of these spatio-temporal concentrations constitutes an 'event,' a place and time at which motion has tended to linger. Once a series of these events has been articulated, they and the steps within them can be compared to each other in meaningful ways, ranging from elementary measurements such as density and duration to more complex properties like repetition and sequence.

Our own remarkable ability to detect and interpret such patterns of observed or simulated movement has motivated the development of fascinating digital tools and techniques for data visualization. As spatio-temporal datasets become larger and more complex, however, the utility of even the most powerful visualization techniques is limited by human faculties that can rapidly become overwhelmed. Whether *we* can see these space-time patterns is no longer the issue; of greater concern now is the question of whether *our computers* can see them.

Digital techniques for the interpretation of spatio-temporal data also have evolved dramatically over the past several decades. Although these techniques are often designed to mimic their human counterparts, computer algorithms tend to function quite differently from human minds. Consider, for example, the fundamental problem of identifying events. What makes this problem both interesting and challenging is that events are much like clouds in the sky; they are emergent, scale-dependent, and fuzzy in both the spatial and temporal dimensions.

As is often the case in designing algorithms, a solution to this problem comes into focus when the problem itself is re-envisioned by turning it inside out. Given a sequence of points that are unevenly situated in space but scheduled at equal intervals of time, each point can be regarded as part of an event. Some of these events

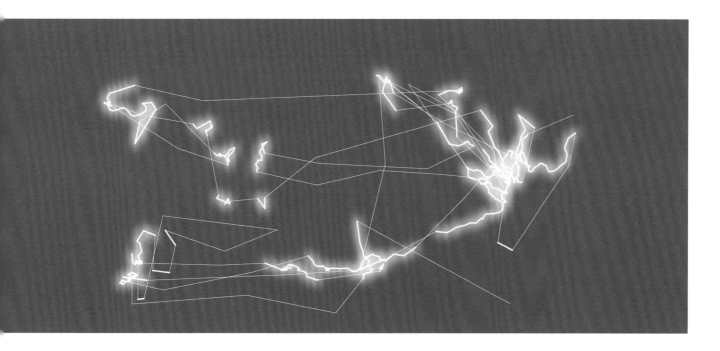

may be fleeting, whereas others are more persistent. The critical notion here is that breaks between consecutive events occur whenever one of those points lands beyond a specified distance away from its immediate predecessors. Furthermore, the crucial element of this critical notion resides in the last letter of its final word—not *predecessor* but *predecessors*. If the distinction between consecutive events were to depend only on distances between consecutive points, there would be no difference between a sizable step directed away from the preceding points (which should initiate a new event) and a sizable step directed back into their midst (which should not). To account for this, each point's distance is measured not from the preceding point, but rather from the centroid of whatever preceding points have occurred within a specified time frame.

Significantly, this straightforward device makes it possible to associate every point with a distinct event, and to do so even before that event has fully emerged. With the ability to specify maximum limits on both distance and time frame, events can also be defined at particular spatial and temporal scales. This makes it possible to distinguish, for example, movement among cities over a span of days from movement among buildings over a span of hours. In either case, what previously seemed fuzzy is thereby translated into discrete events.

Once a series of distinct events has been delineated in this manner, those of fleeting duration can be eliminated, and those that become consecutive as a result can be merged (if spatially coincident) to remove the effects of anomalous 'blips' on otherwise uniform motion. Those that remain can then be visualized as shown in Figure 2.

Each of the thick lines in Figure 2 constitutes an event, and each of these events can now be characterized in terms of properties such as starting time, stopping time, duration,

centroid, and dispersion. Events that lie within a specified spatial vicinity of one another can now also be compiled into meaningful 'sites' like those depicted here as islands of white. Each of these sites can then be characterized in terms of similar properties, as well as new properties such as the number of visits to that site. Once sites have been defined, each event can also be further characterized in terms of additional properties, e.g., its ordinal position among the visits to its site, the time elapsed since the first or the most recent of those visits, and the number or nature of other sites visited in the interim. Each point too can now be further characterized in relation to others from the same event or the same site in order to measure such properties as accumulation or decay over time and deviation in space.

Ultimately, this construct yields a computational language, a clear and coherent vocabulary with which to instruct a digital colleague. Though this may well be a colleague whose data-processing power is tireless, that colleague is also likely to be one for whom a statement like the following would otherwise seem self-contradictory: "We always go to the same place at the same time each year, but we always stay at a different place, and each year we stay a bit longer."

At a time when our ability to affect the world around us is rapidly becoming more and more dependent on digital media, our ability to work creatively with those media often calls for a delicate and fluid balance between precise measurements and imprecise ideas. The language proposed does not attempt to strike that balance *per se*, but it does attempt to establish parameters that will enable its users to do so.

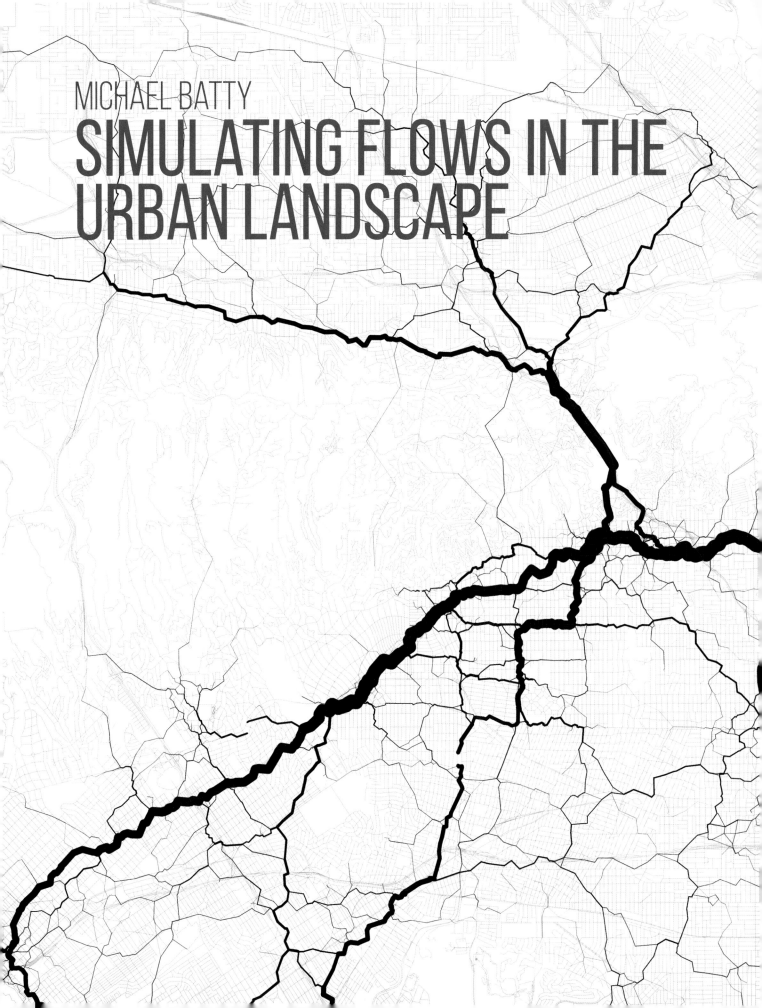

Michael Batty is Bartlett Professor of Planning at University College London where he manages the Centre for Advanced Spatial Analysis (CASA). His book *The New Science of Cities* (2013) summarizes recent work linking urban morphology to computable models of city systems and their physical design. His group is also involved in ideas about smart cities and big data, particularly new visualizations of transport and movement. He is the editor of the journal *Environment and Planning B*.

+ CARTOGRAPHY, SPATIAL ANALYTICS, URBAN STUDIES

The idea that cities can be understood as systems has pervaded our approach to planning and design for well over a century. Patrick Geddes, who imported ideas from biology and the theory of evolution into our understanding of cities, was among the first to suggest that there might be a science of cities that would reflect how cities grow through interactions and movement. But it was Benton MacKaye's conception of flows in the landscape that propelled these ideas forward, introducing an era in which cities were viewed as general systems composed of interacting parts, whose dynamics established configurations that appeared to be in equilibrium while at the same time admitting temporal change.

In his book *The New Exploration*, MacKaye defined how the modern urban landscape was evolving in relation to those of earlier periods.[1] He defined regional landscapes as a synthesis of flows, originating from geological and climatic changes, on which agricultural patterns evolved. MacKaye's model of flows is strangely prescient relative to our current concern for capturing and simulating what is happening in cities. Developments in digital visualization and simulation allow us to articulate and envision complexity in ways that previously could only be imagined. And yet, many designers and planners continue to think of cities as spaces and places, rather than understanding location as a constellation of interactions, a product of relations among people and places. Cities must be conceptualized in terms of patterns of communication, interaction, trade, and exchange rather than as idealized morphologies. Contemporary information technology is the most important driver of our understanding of new forms of flow and flux in urban systems. For the first time, we have the tools to give formal meaning to MacKaye's insights.

MacKaye's model of a developed urban landscape assumes a bounded hinterland or basin that is drained physically by means of what he called its indigenous structure. The flows that characterized this landscape were comprised of everything from water to people, all usually focused on some sink point, often the center of a market, where physical flows discharge. MacKaye called this the *inflow*. In almost symmetrical but opposite fashion, he defined the *outflow* as the movement of people and materials from the market to the hinterland, arguing that these two reversible sets of flows, when balanced, defined a sustainable landscape – a pattern of circular flows mirroring production and consumption. He then argued that this sustainability was in fact being destroyed in contemporary urban

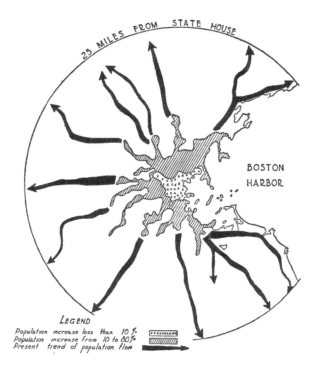

25 MILES FROM STATE HOUSE

BOSTON HARBOR

LEGEND
Population increase less than 10%.
Population increase from 10 to 80%.
Present trend of population flow

systems by a *backflow* that results when too much activity is attracted to the sink – when cities, for example, become so large that their economies of agglomeration disappear and diseconomies of scale set in. In the evolution of such a landscape, MacKaye speaks of a *reflow*, or a subsequent wave of inflow. His model treats any landscape as a complex co-evolution and convolution of these flow patterns – that is, as a succession of inflows and outflows that build successive waves of development.

The processes that create flows must be defined; diffusion is the most obvious process, but attraction, its opposite, is equally important. The models composed of these processes and their resulting networks are abstractions that simplify the ways in which landscapes function and evolve. Like all models, they are only as good as the information that they seek to represent. As such, they serve to represent how cities actually function and how people, materials, information, and energy move and flow to keep our cities working and sustainable. Retaining the multi-dimensional characteristics of flows that define our urban landscapes, however, is challenging. Irrespective of the recent dramatic advances in computer simulation, critical information regarding the attributes that define flows is lost when processes are reduced to locations and singular dimensions.

Within a bounded region, diffusion and attraction seek to use or to fill as much space as possible, so that resources can be delivered throughout the region in the most efficient and parsimonious way. In the case of a population that grows from a source of settlement or market center and then spreads out to maintain a certain density, the growth will take place in successive rings around the source. In fact, to minimize travel distances, it will actually form a tree-like structure, for this is a cost-efficient way to establish links or routes everywhere. In a different context, products from the hinterland needed to sustain the population will flow in the other direction, using similarly parsimonious connections. These patterns co-evolve and cannot be separated; however, to illustrate their formation, they can be simulated individually.

Imagine a source on the landscape, at the confluence of a river, on an estuary, or at some accessible point where the kernel of a settlement is located. If the seed of growth spurts out from there in regular fashion, an increment of population will appear around the source, as if fired from a pop-gun; then, once the population elements land in the hinterland, they begin a random walk to find the embryonic city.

Once an element finds another element that has already stuck (the first time this will be at the seed source), it sticks and another element pops out and begins its random walk. This can be thought of as an agent-based model. This process leads to the creation not of a formless or amorphous mass but of a highly structured dendrite. Branches emerge in the structure because the first time an element sticks, its presence increases the probability of further sticking in the vicinity of that location. This begins a process of 'path dependence.' The structure becomes variegated in fjord-like fashion because, once branches have begun to develop, it is increasingly hard for an element to penetrate between the branches.[2] It sticks before it gets deep into the crevasses, reinforcing the branching structure by this positive feedback. The figures on following pages show a schematic of this process and the ultimate dendritic pattern that develops. This system can be tuned to produce different degrees of space-filling, from quite skeletal structures to much more unorganized masses, by changing the probabilities of sticking.

In countervailing fashion, a process similar to the outflow takes place continually, whereby the hinterland is successively drained of resources to support the population, following routes to the source, which is usually a focus for exchange, a market, or a point of transshipment. Over time, these systems often converge, and the channel capacities are determined in proportion to all the inflows and outflows. The channels that result are often overlaid on each other to enable different transportation modes and also contain other physical systems (e.g., utilities) of many kinds with their own networked infrastructure.

These flow models can be configured in many different ways and tuned to particular situations in which numerous flow patterns all interact and co-evolve. When real urban landscapes are observed, the culmination of these patterns can be generated. Using these diffusion models results in patterns that resemble actual urban landscapes thereby demonstrating that simple bottom-up, local interactions indeed produce highly organized structures. Thus, such models can be used to simulate options for future urban forms.

Flows are the signatures of how the urban landscape functions in terms of its form. The flow patterns illustrated are composites determined over long periods of time, which can also be glimpsed in more routine, diurnal fashion, and they can be generalized to many well-known patterns in nature.[3] We now

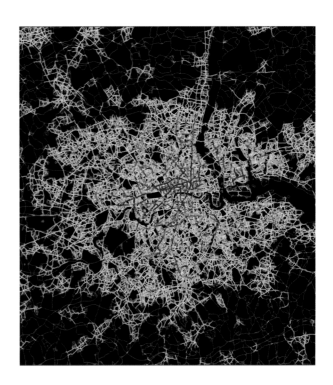

Opposite and Above: Metropolitan urban landscapes structured around various flow systems. Boston Population Outflow image from Benton MacKaye, *The New Exploration: A Philosophy of Regional Planning* (1928) and road traffic flow in London from CASA.

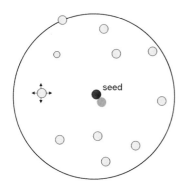

A.

The outflow is generated at the source site (red) and, at each time interval, it generates units of development (blue) that are projected into the periphery. The increment of population then searches for an occupied site, which in the first instance is the seed site, by randomly walking (blue dot showing n-s-e-w directions) across the space. Once it finds the occupied site, it sticks (light red). Another unit is generated and projected into the periphery and the walk begins again. In this way, the city is generated with a dendritic structure.

[B] to [E] is generating a pattern of outflows. [F] to [I] shows variable configurations with different degrees of compactness.

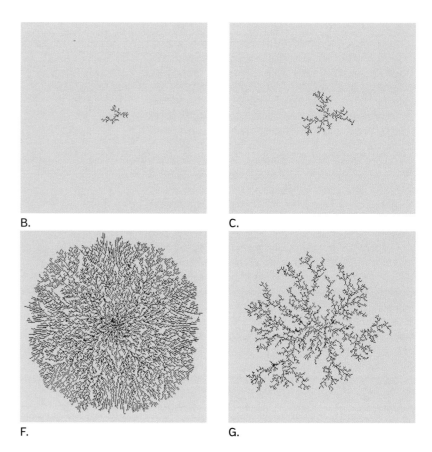

B.

C.

F.

G.

have snapshots of how these flow systems change over time, particularly for daily patterns of physical traffic that can be monitored in real time and documented on a second-by-second basis using various mobile or fixed sensor devices. Physical movements of vehicles and passengers are the easiest flows to collect and sense using automated procedures. For example, smart cards record where people enter and leave a transit system, generating enormous quantities of data, clearly defined with regard to time and location, from which various activity patterns can be extracted.

Now imagine that we have mapped hundreds of these flow patterns (as we actually have done). How all this adds up to the flows that define our living places is the great challenge, for many of them are not clearly visible, some are hidden, and some, of course, are confidential. To explain how cities form and function a comprehensive science must be developed that can embrace this range of understanding.[4] This science will be based on spatial interactions of many kinds, which cover many different spatial scales and temporal periods, reflecting shifts between geographic and geometric representations as well as between fast and slow dynamics.

Although MacKaye envisaged landscapes as flow patterns, he also argued that through observing contemporary urban landscapes in this way these flows could reveal clear problems that regional planning needed to address. He argued that the forces driving metropolitan expansion in early 20th-century urban America were overwhelming any sense of balance in the urban landscape. MacKaye's notion of a balanced cycle of production and consumption—sustainable in spatial terms as the product of inflows and outflows—was being broken by backflows as urban dwellers sought to escape the congestion formed by this imbalance. More recently, as our knowledge of equilibrium in physical systems has grown, the notion of exact balance has been qualified by ideas concerning dynamic equilibria, systems that remain far from equilibrium, and even chaotic states. It is thus not easy to simply visualize flows and draw definitive conclusions about the state of the urban system with respect to the theoretical balance alluded to here.

The critical issue in this style of theorizing and modeling is that different processes lead to similar outcomes. This is defined as equifinality, and landscapes are classic examples of this phenomenon. The models that generate these outcomes are very different from the more deterministic economic and

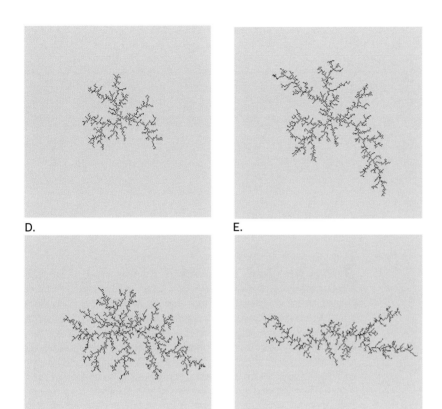

D.

E.

H.

I.

1 Benton MacKaye, *The New Exploration: A Philosophy of Regional Planning* [New York: Harcourt, Brace, and Co., 1928].

2 Michael Batty, *Cities and Complexity* [Cambridge: MIT Press, 2005].

3 Philip Ball, *Flow: Nature's Patterns* [Oxford: Oxford University Press, 2009].

4 Michael Batty, *The New Science of Cities* [Cambridge: MIT Press, 2013].

transportation models that define urban economic structures in which processes of energy and information transfer are largely absent. In developing good models of urban landscapes and their evolution, it is essential to visualize the dynamics of flows through snapshots of what happens through time and across space, and it is necessary to do this over different time horizons – in short, across all spatial and temporal scales. These models lie at the core of urban evolution, and they constitute the essence of urban dynamics and the temporal interpretations of the ways in which traffic systems respond to congestion, capacity, and mode switching at different spatial scales and over different time periods. They also provide ways in which one can explore processes of information transfer in cities, as these processes involve a variety of new flow systems such as finance, social media, and entertainment, all of which contribute to defining the new ways in which cities and their urban landscapes are currently evolving.

Detecting problems in growth and evolution that call for our positive intervention requires longer and more involved discussions; however, today's simulations indicate that the tools to develop urban theories that will help us steer urban landscapes toward more optimal conditions are becoming more widely available. The new field of city science is hard at work developing simulation models that can provide substantive support for planning and design processes. These models, however, are still largely exploratory and need further development. Models are always incomplete, and even good models can still be made more accurate and more relevant. Yet better theory is also needed, and many of the issues raised over the last century by commentators on city planning remain critical. The models introduced must be extended to embrace these concerns, and this need presents a new series of important challenges.

ETIENNE S. BENSON

# MOVEMENT ECOLOGY AND THE MINIMAL ANIMAL

Etienne S. Benson is an Assistant Professor in the Department of History and Sociology of Science at the University of Pennsylvania. He writes about the history of ecology, environmentalism, and human-animal relations and is the author of *Wired Wilderness: Technologies of Tracking and the Making of Modern Wildlife* (2010).

✚ COMPUTER SCIENCES, ECOLOGY, HISTORY

Among ecologists, movement is on the move. Over the past decade or so, a growing number of researchers have begun to focus their attention on how and why individual animals move across landscapes through time. Research programs come and go, and there is no way of knowing how long this new field of movement ecology will retain its promise or what new forms it might take. Nonetheless the emergence of this approach to studying animals and landscapes can tell us something about the way scientific practices and conceptions of the animal are changing in an era of Big Data and of growing concerns about the impact of humanity on global ecological processes.[1]

The term 'movement ecology' is not new in the scientific literature, but it was only with the articulation of a theoretical program by ecologist Ran Nathan in 2008 that it began to be understood as something around which an epistemic community could be organized, generalized theories could be developed, and broad appeals for support could be made.[2] Since then movement ecology has become one of ecology's fastest-growing sub-specialties. Numerous conferences have been held, major grants have been awarded, and journals such as *Movement Ecology* and *Animal Biotelemetry* have been founded. Movement ecologists often attribute the recent expansion of their field to technological advances in communications, surveillance, and computing. Nathan, for example, has written that the rise of movement ecology can be explained in large part by new tracking methods that promise to "revolutionize our understanding of movement phenomena because they allow us to address key questions that we were not able to examine before."[3] Similarly, ornithologist Martin Wikelski has envisioned a future in which satellite-based sensors and animal-borne tags will allow biologists to fill in the "white spaces that we still have on the globe for animal movement" and even to "use animals as distributed sensor networks around the globe."[4] Technology, rather than any particular theoretical insight or empirical discovery, seems to be leading the way.

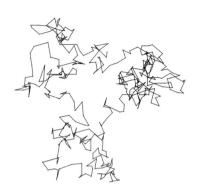

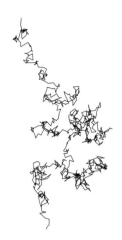

At the same time, as one group of leading movement ecologists has written, "the explosion of data volume and variety has created new challenges and opportunities for information management, integration, and analysis."[5] The perceived urgency of overcoming these challenges originates both from ecologists' desire to work at the cutting edge of their field and from their sense that the Earth faces a crisis of human making. Developing adequate data-analysis and data-management practices has thus become central to at least some ecologists' understanding of their moral obligations as scientists and as environmentalists. This is one reason that theoretical frameworks such as the one proposed by Nathan have been so warmly received. In addition to positioning movement as a legitimate object of ecological inquiry–rather than merely an indicator of more important underlying processes–such frameworks help to discipline and render comparable inherently unwieldy and diverse biological data. For this project, the otherwise distant domain of genomics has frequently served as a comparison. Nathan, for example, writes that the "scientific revolution potentiated by genome sequencing can be compared with insights about movement drawn from mapping every step and stop of an individual during its lifetime track from birth to death."[6] Reduced to a series of locations, the individual's life thus becomes amenable to analysis.

The establishment of centralized data repositories such as Movebank, which currently contains data from more than 2,000 movement ecology studies, is also helping to render manageable the overwhelming amount of movement data now available.[7] As with the pioneering genetics database GenBank, Movebank aims to facilitate the establishment of an international epistemic community around a novel object of study: the movement track, understood as a sequence of latitude-longitude pairs in time.[8] While genomics casts a long shadow over the recent development of movement ecology, there is also a longer history of ecologists' efforts to develop workable models of real-world animal movements – a history that can teach us something about what is at stake in movement ecology's data-management practices and its imagination of animal life. The first digital representations of what movement ecologists call the 'lifetime track' of an animal date to the 1960s, when mainframe computers first became widely available on American university campuses. While mathematical models of animal movement had existed since the early 20th century, digital computers suddenly made it feasible to statistically model the movements and decision-making processes of a single animal. What was probably the world's first digital simulation of animal movement was developed at the University of Minnesota by statistical ecologist Donald B. Siniff in 1967. Titled SIMPLOT, the program was intended less as an accurate representation of animal behavior than as a way of identifying real-world deviations from statistical models. In a way that would have been impossible with real animals moving through real landscapes, it allowed the scientist to experiment with the consequences of his or her own assumptions.[9]

Since the 1960s, efforts to model animal movement in the digital medium of the electronic computer have been powerful accelerators of ecologists' tendencies toward 'behavioral minimalism.' This is a

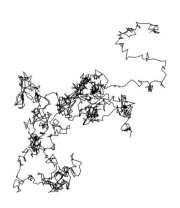 

1 Sabine Leonelli, "What Difference Does Quantity Make? On the Epistemology of Big Data in Biology," *Big Data & Society* 1, no. 1 (2014): 1–11; Christophe Bonneuil & Jean-Baptiste Fressoz, *The Shock of the Anthropocene: The Earth, History, and Us*, trans. David Fernbach (Brooklyn, NY: Verso, 2016).

2 Ran Nathan, et al., "A Movement Ecology Paradigm for Unifying Organismal Movement Research," *Proceedings of the National Academy of Science* 105, no. 49 (9 Dec. 2008): 19052–59.

3 "Ran Nathan on the Growing Importance of Movement Ecology," (October 2010), http://archive.sciencewatch.com/inter/aut/2010/10-oct/10octNath1/ (accessed December 20, 2015).

4 Martin Wikelski, "Move It, Baby!" talk delivered at the 2014 Symposium on Animal Movement and the Environment held at the North Carolina Museum of Natural Sciences in Raleigh, North Carolina, on May 5, 2014, https://www.youtube.com/watch?v=PxtJAXQQU40 (accessed December 20, 2015).

5 Roland Kays, et al., "Terrestrial Animal Tracking as an Eye on Life and Planet," *Science* 348, no. 6240 (12 June 2015), DOI: 10.1126/science.aaa2478.

6 Nathan et al. "A Movement Ecology Paradigm for Unifying Organismal Movement Research," 19053.

7 "About Movebank," https://www.movebank.org/node/2 (accessed December 20, 2015).

8 "BD&I: MoveBank: Integrated Database for Networked Organism Tracking," Award Abstract #0756920, US National Science Foundation, http://www.nsf.gov/awardsearch/showAward?AWD_ID=0756920 (accessed December 20, 2015). On GenBank, see Hallam Stevens, *Life Out of Sequence: A Data-Driven History of Bioinformatics* (Chicago: University of Chicago Press, 2013).

term that ecologists Steven Lima and Patrick Zollner have used to describe a research strategy focused "on only those few behavioral traits that are likely to be important to the question under study."[10] It requires shutting out of view all of the irrelevant factors, which in turn–and this is where things get tricky– requires deciding in advance which factors are relevant or irrelevant. As Lima and Zollner argue, behavioral minimalism is useful and often even necessary; without it, much of the enormous complexity of animal life would remain intractable to scientific inquiry. It becomes problematic, however, when it becomes an ontological claim about what animals and other organisms really are – that is, when a strategy of behavioral minimalism is taken as evidence of the existence of what might be described as "minimal animals."[11] With the help of digital computers, minimal animals have proliferated over the past several decades.

Even as they pursue the strategy of behavioral minimalism described by Lima and Zollner, movement ecologists today are careful to acknowledge the complexity of animal movement. In Nathan's theoretical framework, for example, the individual animal's movement track is conceptualized as the result of environmental, physical, and cognitive processes that cannot be reduced to latitude-longitude pairs. Similarly, Wikelski and others have been careful to leave room in data repositories such as Movebank for other forms of data besides location.[12] Nonetheless, as movement ecologists develop generalized theories with the help of highly abstracted mathematical models, and as they aggregate data about diverse species into central repositories, they are implicitly embracing a data-driven version of behavioral minimalism – one in which the movements of animals become self-evidently comparable to the Brownian motion of particles or the dispersal of seeds by wind.

Behavioral minimalism is nothing new in animal ecology, but the intensity with which it is now being pursued and the extent to which it is dependent on a particular set of research technologies is unprecedented. However sophisticated their underlying models may be, most studies by movement ecologists focus on the landscape-scale movements that are easily observed with modern tracking techniques. Factors that are harder to measure and to model become secondary considerations: at best 'annotations' around the scaffolding provided by location data, at worst endlessly deferred desiderata for some future experiment. Similarly, the desire to develop models and build data repositories that work for any species in any environment has

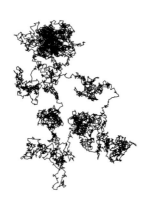

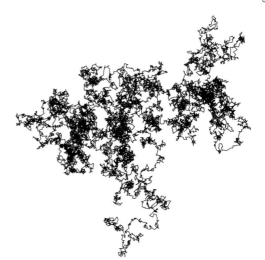

encouraged a reduction of the phenomenon of movement to the lowest common denominator, the latitude-longitude pair. By focusing on tracking methods that produce enormous amounts of data at ever-lower costs, movement ecologists are implicitly adopting a locational form of behavioral minimalism as the ontological foundation of their work.

In the long run this may prove to be a risky path toward scientific success, even judging by the narrowest of criteria. A few years ago, biologists Alistair Boettiger and George Wittemyer and their colleagues conducted a movement-ecology study of African elephants in northern Kenya. Using a mathematical model derived from signal processing theory, remote-sensing data from satellites, and movement data collected with GPS collars, they were able to predict elephant movements on the basis of landscape features as well as past behavior. One of their findings was that the incorporation of landscape and behavior significantly improved the accuracy of the prediction, but only in areas relatively unaffected by human activity. When the elephants moved through human-dominated areas, the accuracy of the prediction fell dramatically, "probably because movement behavior was reactive to the presence, movements, and threats of humans and livestock in such areas."[13]

This is a conclusion that seems likely to be relevant well beyond the specifics of the particular landscapes and animals under study, and it is one that suggests the limits of a minimalistic approach to animal movement that is driven primarily by the technological affordances of present-day tracking and computing technologies. The increasing human domination of the planet is precisely the reason that the theoretical models and central data repositories of movement ecology seem so urgent; it is also the reason that ecologists' models may become less and less predictive over time, no matter how much location data they are able to collect. Technological affordances and theoretical frameworks may run up against the contingencies of history, which is increasingly rendering chimerical the idea of a 'human-free zone' of precise prediction. In that case, movement ecologists may want to consider incorporating other methods that can articulate the movement of animals across landscapes in an idiom richer and wider than a series of points on a map.[14]

9 On the context in which Siniff developed SIMPLOT, see Etienne Benson, *Wired Wilderness: Technologies of Tracking and the Making of Modern Wildlife* (Baltimore: Johns Hopkins University Press, 2010), 5–51. A live version of the program is available at http://etiennebenson.com/simplot/.

10 Steven L. Lima & Patrick A. Zollner, "Towards a Behavioral Ecology of Ecological Landscapes," *Trends in Ecology and Evolution* 11, no. 3 (March 1996): 132–35, 133.

11 Etienne Benson, "Minimal Animal: Surveillance, Simulation, and Stochasticity in Wildlife Biology," *Antennae: The Journal of Nature in Visual Culture* 30 (Winter 2014): 39–53.

12 In 2013, Wikelski and his colleagues introduced a software tool called Env-DATA that simplifies the process of matching animal movements to the environmental factors that may be influencing them. Somayeh Dodge, et al., "The Environmental-data Automated Track Annotation (Env-DATA) System: Linking Animal Tracks with Environmental Data," *Movement Ecology* 1, no. 3 (December 2013), http://www.movementecologyjournal.com/content/1/1/3.

13 Alistair N. Boettiger, et al., "Inferring Ecological and Behavioral Drivers of African Elephant Movement Using a Linear Filtering Approach," *Ecology* 92, No. 8 (August 2011), 1648–57, 1656.

14 S. Eben Kirksey & Stefan Helmreich, "The Emergence of Multispecies Ethnography," *Cultural Anthropology* 25 (2010): 545–76.

Previous pages and above: The end results of the SIMPLOT algorithm with run lengths ranging from 10 to 20,000 steps.

# GARBAGE OUT, GARBAGE IN

In 1957, the world's first satellite was launched into space. Now almost six decades later, space is replete with junk. NASA recently calculated that there are more than 700,000 objects of 1 cm or larger in low Earth orbit. While seemingly miniscule, space debris travels at twice the speed of active craft and fragments larger than 1 mm in size pose a serious collision hazard. This space junk also poses a threat to earthbound humans; nearly 100 tons of debris falls to the earth each year. NASA initiated the Orbital Debris Program in 1972 to develop simulation models that assess the risk presented by orbital debris to operating spacecraft and to predict future Earth reentry. These mathematical models have repeatedly shown that debris in low orbit will continue to increase irrespective of whether new objects are launched into space. With large collisions occurring every five to ten years, the increasing space clutter will make tracking and avoiding the debris even more complicated and costly.

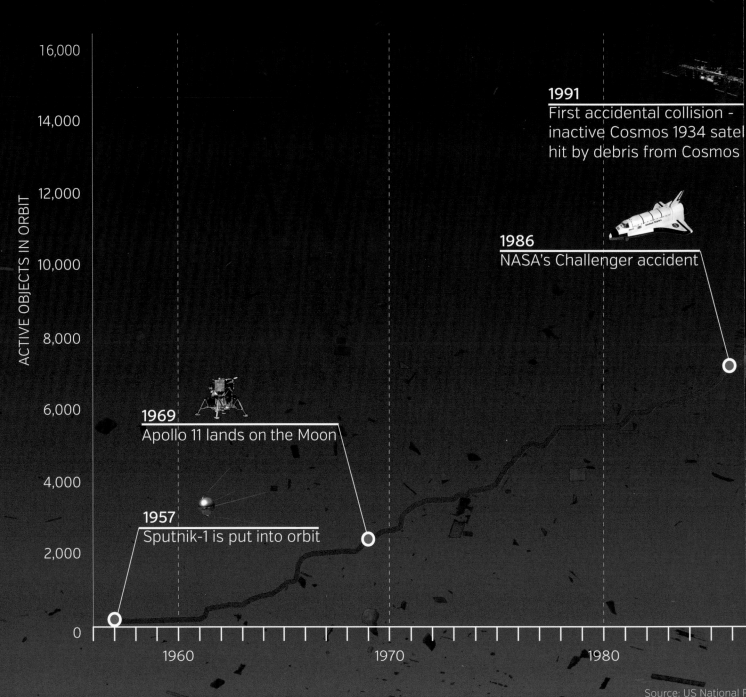

**1991**
First accidental collision - inactive Cosmos 1934 satel hit by debris from Cosmos

**1986**
NASA's Challenger accident

**1969**
Apollo 11 lands on the Moon

**1957**
Sputnik-1 is put into orbit

ACTIVE OBJECTS IN ORBIT

16,000
14,000
12,000
10,000
8,000
6,000
4,000
2,000
0

1960     1970     1980

Source: US National F

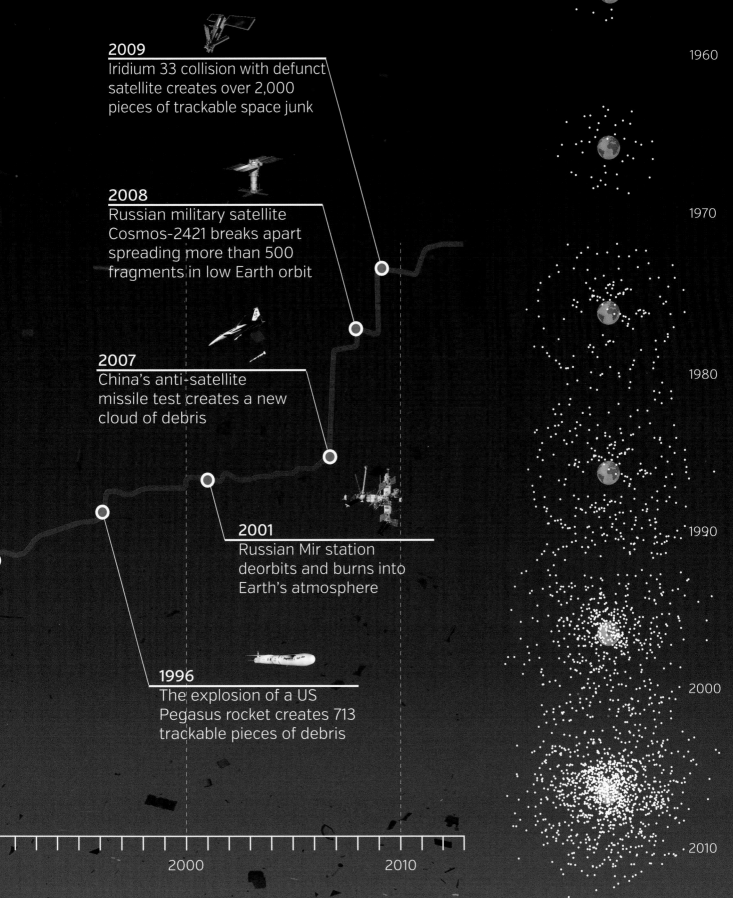

**2009**
Iridium 33 collision with defunct satellite creates over 2,000 pieces of trackable space junk

**2008**
Russian military satellite Cosmos-2421 breaks apart spreading more than 500 fragments in low Earth orbit

**2007**
China's anti-satellite missile test creates a new cloud of debris

**2001**
Russian Mir station deorbits and burns into Earth's atmosphere

**1996**
The explosion of a US Pegasus rocket creates 713 trackable pieces of debris

1960
1970
1980
1990
2000
2010

2000
2010

NASA Orbital Debris Program Office, United Nations Office for Outer Space Affairs, Orbital Debris Quarterly NewsNational Geographic, satellitedebris.net.

**Eric Winsberg** is Professor of Philosophy at the University of South Florida. He has been writing about philosophical issues surrounding computer simulation for almost two decades, including the book *Science in the Age of Computer Simulation*. He also writes on climate science, statistical mechanics and the arrow of time, and on theories of truth. Eric has degrees in the History, Philosophy, and Social Studies of Science and Medicine and a PhD in the History and Philosophy of Science. We spoke with Eric about the impact of simulation on the nature of scientific evidence, its implications for policy, and what he sees as the most pertinent uses of simulation today.

+ How would you define simulation in the context of your work?

In a very narrow sense, a simulation is when you run a program on a computer using step-by-step methods to explore the approximate behavior of a mathematical model. Usually that's a mathematical model of some real world system. You give the computer some initial state of the system and it calculates the system's state over and over again, which gives you a numerical picture of the system's behavior. Second, computer simulation is a comprehensive method for studying systems. In this broader sense, the computer simulation is an entire process. It's the process of choosing the model, finding a way to implement that model in a form that you can run on the computer, calculating the output, and checking to see if that output looks reasonable or if it agrees with data that you already have. If it doesn't, you may go back and modify the model or you go back and modify the way that you implemented the model on the computer. Then you visualize and study the data, you draw conclusions out of that, and you make arguments for the reliability of those conclusions.

The third definition involves what it means to simulate more broadly. Simulation is whenever you have a target system that you're interested in and a source system that you think, for whatever reason, imitates that target system well enough so that by studying the source system you can learn about the target system. If the source system is a computer, then it's computer simulation.

+ Originally, the notion of something enduring and authentic lies on the other side of a simulation. If we no longer hold this to be true, how does this alter how we understand the mediating role of simulation to operate?

I tend to think that what lies on the other side of simulation is direct observation or intervention. If I want to learn about how a cockroach behaves and I watch it or I poke at it, that's the opposite of simulation. Simulation, as I previously said in the third definition, is when I have a surrogate. So, surrogacy is in a way what lies on the other side–is what is characteristic of simulation. But I do not think surrogacy is the opposite of endurance or authenticity. Authenticity is the opposite of forgery or fake or copy. Simulation is a kind of copy or forgery but I don't think authenticity is particularly important from an epistemological point of view. It could be one reason for thinking you've got an epistemologically good strategy but I don't think it's required. I could have a really good forgery of a Rembrandt and I could use that to learn perfectly good things about Rembrandt's style or his technique or his composition or his brush stroke. So, if I want to learn about something and I've got a good forgery, that's perfectly okay.

+ We could say, very broadly, that scientists and designers use computer simulation differently: the scientists use it for more descriptive and explanatory purposes–how the world 'is'– and the designers for more exploratory purposes–how the world can be modified. However, at least in climate modeling, we are seeing a culture of 'play' in science. Scientists are using simulation in 'what if' scenarios as a way to explore the implications and consequences of climatic trends. What epistemological questions does this raise for philosophers of science?

I want to challenge one of the presuppositions of the question. I'm reluctant to accept the dichotomy between description and exploration being suggested here. One of the best cases for breaking down this dichotomy is the enormous amount of exploration that is required when studying complex systems. If you want to understand a complex physical system, one of the first things that you do is to explore lots and lots of simulation runs to see how it responds to different possible inputs. You want to get what one climate scientist calls 'process understanding' where you get a feel for what are the main variables that drive the behavior of the system. In a really complex system, there are going to be many variables, some of which, if you change them, will not make very much difference. Other changes, however, will propagate with enormous causal impact. The way that you learn is via this exploration or play or 'what if' scenarios. And, again, in climate science, we want to make projections of what will happen in various different urban scenarios and that's a predictive task really but it also requires this kind of exploration.

+ Some have called simulations a third way of doing science in that it is neither theoretical nor experimental. Do you agree? If so, then might you reflect on the significance of this and its relation to science entering a 'post-empirical' age? When or how do the results of a simulation achieve their own authority if they aren't based on observable phenomena?

I'm not a huge fan of the expression that simulations are a third way of doing science, in part because all simulations have aspects to them that are theoretical and all have aspects that are experimental. But a more important reason is that science is always expanding its toolkit. In the 17th century we developed calculus, in the 19th century statistical methods and, in the early 20th century, time series analysis, which is incredibly important for the study of complex systems. More recently we've started using machine learning and 'big data.' Analog simulations, which I've started writing about more recently, is another addition to the scientific toolkit. So, there isn't one or two or three ways of doing science.

I think, in general, this expression of a post-empirical science is based on a naïve conception of the relation between theory and data. It makes it seem as though there's a kind of black and white divide between theories that make hypotheses and theories that make a direct connection with the world. But the question of what mediates between theory and data has always been complicated. Maybe the mediation is getting more and more complex as we get into more rarified areas of science but I don't think there's ever been a line in the sand.

+ Could you expand a little more on what you mean by analog simulations?

Earlier, I defined simulation as whenever you have some source system that you've studied because you hope it resembles a target system well enough. Many times that's a computer, but it needn't be so. For example, Radin Dardashti, Karim Thébault, and I have recently been working on looking at what are called dumb hole simulations, which is when physicists are interested in testing the prediction that Stephen Hawking made in the 1970s that black holes radiate because of the effects of quantum mechanics in curved space time. What William Unruh suggested was that you could actually study that question by setting up the right kinds of fluid mechanical apparatus in the laboratory. By setting them up in just the right way so that you had a good argument that their behavior would mirror the behavior of a black hole, you could actually test the hypothesis that black holes radiate. That's an analog simulation.

+ As landscape architects, we rely heavily on images and drawings that represent and translate ideas and concepts into something understandable and relatable to a broader audience. You write about the role of the image in simulation, describing it as an interpretive tool used to make inferences from data, and draw comparisons between simulation results and real systems. Can you speak to the importance of creating representations that resemble the reality they seek to describe compared to the mathematical equations that describe behavior, for example?

The thing that's important to keep in mind on that question is often times we're using computer simulation because the right kind of equations are lacking. The sense in which they're lacking is that physics, for example, typically gives us equations that tell us rates of change. The equations don't tell us behaviors. They give us differential equations and sometimes differential equations are nice to us and we can write down closed form solutions to them. That is to say, we can write down equations that do describe the behavior because they are solutions to the rate of change equations. When we have that it's terrific because those equations are beautiful summaries of everything we know about the system. When we don't have closed form solutions we use simulations. Simulations don't give us anything right away that's even comparable to the kind of power that closed form solution equations give us. Rather, simulations give us big hard drives full of data that aren't really humanly digestible. That's when visualization becomes particularly important to scientists, because it's a way of making the results of simulation humanly cognitively digestible. I think there's probably a bit of difference in how scientists are using visualization compared to how landscape architects are using it.

+ Simulations sometimes incorporate fictions [equations or algorithms that are known to be false, such as 'artificial viscosity'] in order to model the physical phenomena they seek to explain. How do simulations function in explanatory or predictive ways if these fictions exist? Do the fictions in simulations function differently from other forms of representation in the making of knowledge? What 'proof' is there that fiction in science is not science fiction?

The proof is always in the pudding. The proof of the reliability of any kind of representation is always that it has a relevantly good track record of success. So, I don't think it's that different when it comes to employing what I call fictions in simulation. You always want some track record of success that brings the right kind of epistemic credentials to whatever tool you're using out of the toolkit of science. I think what makes fictions in simulation extra difficult is that fictions are typically there to provide compensating errors. You mentioned artificial viscosity in fluid flows of shockwaves. Those are there to compensate for the fact that the simulation is going to be really bad at getting what's going on in a thin shockwave because it fits inside the grid. So you create this compensating error of stretching that shock out to be a little bit thicker so that it'll cover more than a few grid cells. Of course the problem when dealing with compensating errors is that it's hard to know if those errors will keep coming close enough to cancel out in a domain that hasn't yet been looked at. So, that makes establishing the credentials by having the right kind of track record of success more difficult than it is when you don't have compensating errors. But the right pattern of success can give you credentials even when you're in that kind of domain.

+ Given the increase in major damaging storms and floods, there's been a recent surge of interest in uncertainty and risk in design, planning, and engineering. This parallels the upturn in uncertainty quantification in visualization and climate modeling. Can you explain why uncertainty quantification is so important to decision-making processes in policy and planning?

I think uncertainty quantification is extremely important because it can be coupled to our preferences via decision rules. It allows us to separate epistemic expertise on the one hand from judgements of taste, values, or utilities on the other. Whenever we make policy decisions we have to balance costs against benefits – like the cost of building a seawall around Manhattan against the benefit of not drowning if sea level rises too much. To make that judgement, you also have to have a sense of whether it will flood or not. But you also have to know how much you prefer staying dry to spending the money on a seawall.

By delivering probabilities and quantifying uncertainties, experts like climate scientists can give us half of the equation without imposing their own values about what's more important – safety or cost or economic development, and so on. Being able to deliver quantified uncertainties is an extremely powerful tool. It helps us to make decisions rationally but it also enables scientists to allow the consumers of their knowledge to make the decisions about value, utility or taste. Unfortunately, when it comes to very complex systems our very best models outstrip the expertise of any single expert. Climate models are like that. They are built by a wide variety of different people with different expert skillsets. It becomes very hard for experts to quantify uncertainties in the models. That's unfortunate but we're going to have to try to muddle our way through.

+ What do you consider to be the most pertinent issue to which simulation could have the greatest contribution, other than climate models?

The biggest issue that we're confronting in the world today is climate change and so climate forecasting will remain crucial. But simulation is also a really powerful tool to mitigate climate change by using it to design systems that are more energy efficient. People always think of transportation when they think of carbon emissions, but buildings are actually a much larger contributor. If we continue to expand our design toolkit to better simulate the behavior, both of the external environment and of the occupants of buildings, we could make huge strides in energy efficiency.

Jillian Walliss has over 15 years' experience as a landscape architecture academic in Australia and New Zealand. She works in the Landscape Architecture program at the University of Melbourne where she teaches landscape theory and design studios. Walliss' research focuses on the relationship between theory, culture, and contemporary design practice. Her most recent publication, co-authored with Heike Rahmann, is *Landscape Architecture and Digital Technologies: Re-conceptualising Design and Making* (2016).

Heike Rahmann is a landscape architect at RMIT University, Melbourne, Australia, and has worked with various practices within the fields of landscape architecture and urban design in Germany, Japan, and Australia. Her research explores the intersection of landscape, technology, and contemporary urbanism with a focus on design practice and theory. Her publications include the co-authored book *Tokyo Void: Possibilities in Absence* (2014), which examines notions of vacancy and transformation processes in one of the largest urban areas in the world.

✚ CLIMATOLOGY, TECHNOLOGY

Astronaut William Anders' photograph *Earthrise*, taken in 1968 as part of the Apollo 8 mission, is recognized as one of the most influential environmental photographs ever produced. Ian McHarg in *Design with Nature* features the seductive aerial images from the Apollo mission to support his argument for a more holistic and systematic approach to planning, premised on ecological values and analysis. Writing in 1990, James Corner highlighted the contradictory valuation of these compelling aerial images, arguing that they simultaneously represent "both humility and a sense of omnipotent power."[1] Throughout the 1990s, Corner and his contemporaries railed against the totalizing representations of aerial photography and maps, linking these techniques with the rationale and utilitarian measures that were driving the planning and design of cities. Instead, they argued for the re-insertion of imagination and meaning into design processes, bringing a stronger cultural imperative to the landscape project.

Thirty years later, big data and the potential offered by computer simulation have once again enticed landscape architecture into the realm of measurement and technology. Should we consider this a return to the ambitions of the enlightenment project according to

JILLIAN WALLISS + HEIKE RAHMANN

# THE EXPERIMENTAL NATURE OF SIMULATION

which nature can be mastered through measurement and prediction, or does simulation in the 21st century offer alternative possibilities?

We argue that the value of simulation lies not in its replication of reality, but instead in its transformative powers in relation to knowledge. Simulation requires the designer to adopt an experimental process with clearly defined relationships and interdependencies between phenomena and information. Rather than just a predictor of outcomes, simulation can best be described as a controlled discovery, offering a valuable technique for exploring and experimenting for a future shaped by the unpredictability of climate change.

## Climate change as mobilizer

The terms 'climate' and 'landscape' are fundamentally linked, physically and imaginatively. Climate, like landscape, operates across multiple scales and is understood as a mix of physical and cultural characteristics that defy singular definition or measurement. For example, environmental scientist Mike Hulme highlights climate's twin meanings that span "the meteorological and metaphorical," while in a similar manner James Corner defines landscape as "both a spatial milieu and cultural image."[2] However, as we move further into the 21st century, it seems that discourses of landscape have somewhat stalled; they are bound within discussions of representation or landscape-ecological urbanism. In contrast, the concept of the Anthropocene has emerged as a powerful mobilizing idea for philosophers, cultural theorists, scientists, and designers, promoting the re-evaluation of theory and practice.

Intertwining philosophy, science, and design, climate change discourse offers great potential to reinvigorate landscape architecture's theoretical realm and design techniques, especially when considered alongside the computational possibilities of simulation. Currently, landscape architects tend to focus on the problems presented by climate change, bypassing broader philosophical and theoretical questions. But as architecture theorist Etienne Turpin has emphasized, the renewed interrogation of the division of nature and culture presented by the Anthropocene provokes theorists and designers to develop "problem formations adequate to the politics of hyper-complexity" that underpin climate change.[3] Turpin reminds us that "problem-formation is a fundamental task of philosophy," citing Deleuze's well-known phrase that "problems get the solutions they deserve according to the terms by which they are created as problems."[4]

Heat map on site

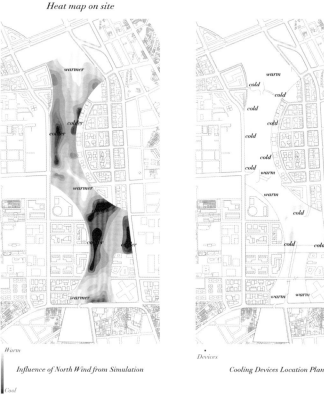

*Wind velocity*
*3.0 m/s*

**North Wind Speed Simulation**

*Wind velocity*
*0.0 m/s*

*Warm*

**Influence of North Wind from Simulation**

*Cool*

*Devices*

**Cooling Devices Location Plan**

Similar to an experiment, simulation requires a clear articulation of problem formation defined through parameters of influence. As such, simulation offers designers new methods for engaging with the hyper-complexity of climate change and with the invisible and dynamic forces that underpin change. In this context, simulation does not provide solutions but instead offers a medium that generates rules and limits to guide design decisions.

Over the last decade, research in computer science has discussed the relationship among simulation, theory, and experiment, arguing that simulation shares characteristics of both theoretical and experimental explorations.[5] The latter model provides a particularly powerful metaphor for design in which simulation becomes an active generator of ideas responsive to changing behaviors, extending into new possibilities that can be tested through multiple parameters. Simulation enables a significant departure from site investigation techniques based on maps or diagrams that are often championed in landscape architecture. These more static techniques offer a visual representation of information and position the designer to respond to what is already known or what can be visually discerned.

The reliance on information–previously processed data shaped by interpretation, meaning, and context–therefore limits the agency of the map or diagram.

In contrast, computational simulations model knowledge based on measurable data rather than information, requiring the active identification of specific parameters or conditions and an understanding of their relations to each other. Simulation relies on identifying a principal model "that characterizes the system in terms of both the arrangement of its constituent parts, and the rules of evolution that govern the changes of state that the system undergoes over time."[6] Instead of relying on observations based on static representation of the past, simulations project into the future and can be conceived as time-based investigations in which change is implicit; they are presented not as an open-ended set of possibilities but, rather, as an active composition of behaviors and relationships.

This significant representational revision fundamentally extends the type and accuracy of information considered within the realm of

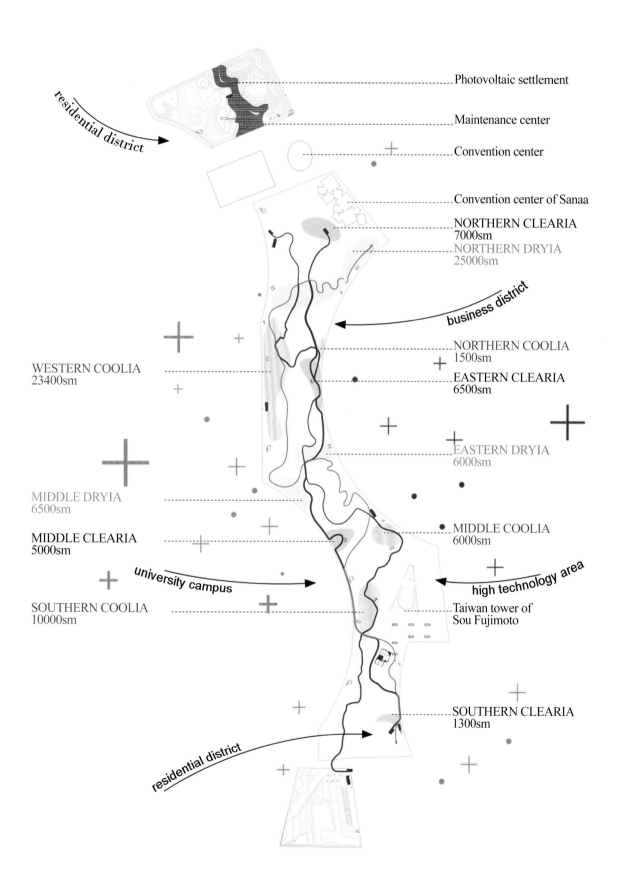

residential district

Photovoltaic settlement

Maintenance center

Convention center

Convention center of Sanaa

NORTHERN CLEARIA
7000sm

NORTHERN DRYIA
25000sm

business district

NORTHERN COOLIA
1500sm

EASTERN CLEARIA
6500sm

WESTERN COOLIA
23400sm

EASTERN DRYIA
6000sm

MIDDLE DRYIA
6500sm

MIDDLE COOLIA
6000sm

MIDDLE CLEARIA
5000sm

university campus

high technology area

Taiwan tower of
Sou Fujimoto

SOUTHERN COOLIA
10000sm

SOUTHERN CLEARIA
1300sm

residential district

site-based investigations. Sensor-based data collection, which can record and measure intangible characteristics of space–such as humidity, illuminance, radiation, temperature, and pressure–offers alternative modes for conceiving sites beyond the standard GIS data techniques that privilege surface-based data and the visuality of site analysis.[7] A direct connection between the site (as data) and a digital simulation encourage a fluid, non-linear feedback loop among analysis, simulation, and design. Consequently, simulation techniques give designers new ways to conceptualize a site not in an absolute form but instead as a prototype that incorporates change, transforming the traditional site survey into a strategy of site surveillance.[8]

In addition, the forces and factors of climate change present designers with new design materialities in the form of atmospheric phenomena. A new generation of designers is departing from a focus on surface factors to question the environmental and social politics of air quality, the bio-politics of atmosphere, the individual's relationship to modified environments, and the fundamental premise of space as bounded territory or surface. Within these design explorations, behavioral properties produce new possibilities for aesthetic values, form, and spatial typologies. Designers are now working at this intersection of technology, science, and nature to explore the complementary potentials of biological

and technological performance. Philippe Rahm and Catherine Mosbach's design for Phase Shifts Park (Taichung, Taiwan) reflects this approach, merging technologically driven climatic devices with the detailed consideration of surface characteristics and planting design to improve the inhabitability of open space. Computational simulation combined with real-time data provides essential techniques for engaging this new theoretical terrain.

As with any form of representation, designers must remain critical in their application of simulations, not defaulting unquestioningly to simulation results. However, digital simulations clearly carry great value in extending a designer's understanding of the performance of designed systems and space. Enabled by computational simulation, the focus on phenomena as new design material marks a shift transcending traditional design techniques and conceptual framings of nature. Attention moves from mediation to amplification of climate through strengthening and augmenting "parameters associated with climate (pressure, temperature, humidity, solar radiation and precipitation) that become initiators of design."[9]

This focus on the performative potentials of climatic conditions underpins the atmospheric design for Phase Shifts Park. Aiming to achieve a healthier and more comfortable outdoor environment, the designers do not seek to achieve absolutes or to modulate conditions, such as by making the hotter areas cooler. Instead, the scheme maintains and even extends the gradation of conditions, established through computer fluid dynamic (CFD) simulations, augmenting qualities where areas are naturally cooler, less polluted, and less humid. Consequently, this tactic is more than a pragmatic response; it is instead guided by Rahm's interest in designing space through voids, particles, and atmospheres rather than through lines and forms. The augmentation of microclimatic parameters amplifies the polarity of conditions, with hot spaces necessary to establish cool ones, thereby "creating spaces by acting on difference."[10] Space emerges through the transformative boundaries of atmospheres and conditions, not as hard spatial delineations. The resulting areas of the park, referred to as Coolia, Dryia, and Clearia, establish an atmospheric structure for the park, with circulation systems conceived to link similar climatic lands.

Through modeling, amplifying, and testing climatic phenomena, parameters, and functions, Phase Shifts Park demonstrates the value of new operative design techniques, which utilize the processing and coding power provided by computer simulations to explore complex systems. At one level, these approaches resemble McHarg's vision of a more holistic and systemic approach to design and planning, with Corner even suggesting that the current data-rich period is a McHargian dream world in which we have access to all the information necessary to propose the right outcome. In fact, contemporary simulations reflect the opposite, as the simulation is able only to suggest the event, not the outcome, and the data fed into the simulation model show the behavior of the parameters, not their optimal state.

This capacity to engage with change demonstrates the immense value of simulation to landscape architecture. Contemporary discourses of ecology and environmental science have significantly altered a Western understanding of nature, embracing human interaction as a fundamental shaping principle of the environment. Concepts of complexity, dynamism, adaptability, and resilience encourage designers to explore "a reorganization of the system's structures and functions into a new or alternative steady state."[11] By modeling systemic relationships, simulations recast understandings of sites from context to dynamic prototype. Within this framing, designers can conceive and test the properties, behaviors, and relationships of systems and phenomena, thereby integrating and speculating on change directly within the design process. Simulation introduces an evidence-based metric into design processes that heightens the biological and technological performance of landscapes and provides quantitative and qualitative arguments for the value of parks, gardens, and green infrastructure. Yet, instead of seeking truth and measurable outcomes that master nature, simulations inform experimental design explorations. Positioned against the contemporary concerns of climate change, simulation promotes controlled discovery and gives agency to new speculations that question the environmental and social politics of air, the individual's relationship to modified environments, and new interpretations of space and experience.

1 James Corner, "Aerial Representation: Irony and Contradiction in an Age of Precision, 1996," in James Corner & Alison Bick Hirsch [eds] *The Landscape Imagination: Collected Essays of James Corner 1990–2010* [New York: Princeton Architectural Press, 2014], 135.

2 See Mike Hulme, *Why We Disagree about Climate Change: Understanding Controversy, Inaction and Opportunity* [Cambridge: Cambridge University Press, 2009], 11; James Corner, "Introduction: Recovering Landscape as a Critical Cultural Practice," in James Corner [ed] *Recovering Landscape: Essays in Contemporary Landscape Architecture* [New York: Princeton Architectural Press, 1999], 5.

3 Etienne Turpin, "Introduction: Who Does the Earth Think It Is, Now?," in Etienne Turpin [ed] *Architecture in the Anthropocene: Encounters among Design, Deep Time, Science and Philosophy* [Ann Arbor, MI: Open Humanities Press, 2013], 1–2.

4 Ibid.

5 Eric Winsberg, "Simulated Experiments: Methodology for a Virtual World," *Philosophy of Science* 70 [2003]: 105.

6 Ibid., 108.

7 Luis Fraguada, et al., "Synchronous Horizons: Redefining Spatial Design in Landscape Architecture through Ambient Data Collection and Volumetric Manipulations," in *ACADIA: Synthetic Digital Ecologies* [San Francisco, CA: Association for Computer-Aided Design in Architecture, 2012], 356.

8 Brian Osborn, *Surveillance Practices: Graduate Option Studio* [University of Virginia, School of Architecture, 2014].

9 Sean Lally, *The Air from Other Planets: A Brief History of Architecture to Come* [Zurich: Lars Müller, 2014], 36.

10 Philippe Rahm, interview with authors at Harvard Graduate School of Design, December 14, 2014.

11 Chris Reed & Nina-Marie Lister [eds], *Projective Ecologies* [Harvard: Actar with Harvard Graduate School of Design, 2014], 276.

Previous page, left: Computer fluid dynamic simulations of pollution, heat, and humidity are used to establish a spatial framework of microclimatic gradients.

Previous page, right: Coolia, Dryia, and Clearia mark areas where climatic parameters for each phenomenon are augmented to expand the microclimatic experience.

Opposite: Artificial and natural devices further amplify comfort levels through purifying, cooling, or dehumidifying existing conditions.

# MARK NYSTROM
# WIND DRAWING

**Mark Nystrom** is an artist and designer whose work explores poetic visualizations of complex information through drawings, installations, and projections. His work has been shown in Austin, Boston, New York, Philadelphia, and other cities across the United States. He is currently an Associate Professor of Graphic Design at Appalachian State University in Boone, North Carolina.

➕ DESIGN, VISUAL ARTS

Mark Nystrom's venture into wind drawings began when he spotted an oak leaf with its stalk wedged in the snow; as the leaf's edges were blown by the wind, it 'drew' a pattern. Inspired, Nystrom attached a ballpoint pen to sails and, placing the apparatus over a piece of paper, recorded shifts in wind speed and direction. He repeated the process for 34 days. Curiosity about the forces that made these drawings led Nystrom to develop digital drawings processes using data collected from weather instruments that he outfits with custom electronics. Nystrom 'sketches' with this data by writing software to interpret it. The resultant drawings are shaped by time, wind speed, and wind direction.

The process shown on the opposite page was the result of Nystrom's work with SP Weather Station, an interdisciplinary project based in New York where 'interpreters' create artworks using one month of weather data. These drawings began with data collected in the first second of the day, marked by a point located in the center of the drawing. The point is pushed away from the center based on wind conditions at the time of data collection. For example, winds from the east will push the point left, and faster winds will push the point further from the center than will slower winds. This process marks the point for the next second's data and a series of lines are drawn between the two points. This recursive process continues each second until all of the day's data has been interpreted. To date, Nystrom has completed 32 digital series based on wind.

September 10, 2010 Greensboro, NC

September 15, 2010 Greensboro, NC

September 25, 2010 Greensboro, NC

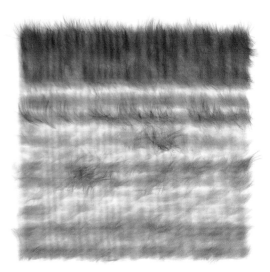

September 29, 2010 Greensboro, NC

September 23, 2010 Greensboro, NC

September 24, 2010 Greensboro, NC

September 30, 2010 Greensboro, NC

October 1,  2010 Greensboro, NC

# CHRISTOPHE GIROT + PHILIPP R.W. URECH
# SIMULATION AS MODEL

Christophe Girot is Professor and Chair of Landscape Architecture at the Department of Architecture of the ETH in Zürich. Prior to joining the ETH in 2001, he chaired Landscape Design at the Versailles School of Landscape Architecture from 1990–2000. His research interests are topological methods in landscape design, landscape perception through new media, and contemporary theory of landscape architecture. His practice in Zürich focuses on large-scale projects in landscape architecture.

Philipp R.W. Urech is a Zürich-based architect. Since 2010 he has collaborated with Christophe Girot at the ETH Department of Architecture, teaching architectural and landscape architectural design in the diploma and post graduate programs, and developing modeling and visualization techniques for elective courses.

+ HYDROLOGY, PLANNING

Opposite: Rendered view of a 3D model of a new park for the Ciliwung River Park in central Jakarta, produced for public presentation.

The meaning of simulation has changed; it has gradually moved from mimicking reality toward an objective expression of a reality. As a result of this semantic shift, one could argue that there is no longer a clear distinction between a model and its copy. With the advent of geo-referentially enabled digital modeling in landscape architecture, the two have almost become one and the same.

There has been a marked evolution in Western thinking since Plato defined mimesis simply as the representation of nature.[1] During the 20th century, philosophers became especially circumspect about the notion of mimesis as something identical to reality. In his text on aesthetic theory, Theodor Adorno clearly frames the question of mimesis differently, stating that the mimetic moment remains identical to itself and bears no resemblance to the world out there.[2] To explain this point of view further, when Walt Disney draws an animated forest in *Snow White* he brings the viewer into full mimesis, in the sense that his forest bears no relationship with any given natural reality. The importance of mimesis is that it is always a self-contained form of imitation, framing only one particular fragment of a total reality capable of making us believe, within bounds, that it is true.

The same characteristic applies to modeling, which has evolved differently depending on the purpose of the inquiry. For a hydraulic engineer, modeling a river involves representing the temporal flow of water in four dimensions within a given physical reality. These models are unlike the three-dimensional physical models typically used in landscape planning and design. The commonality between these different fields of inquiry is the digital terrain model generated from geolocated points, which produce models of great accuracy in the x, y, and z axes. Within a digital terrain model, several operations can take place that test either the flow within an existing situation or potential improvements offered by designs. For example, researchers at the Future Cities Laboratory of the Swiss Federal Institute of Technology (ETH) experimented with designed models of a segment of the Ciliwung River in Jakarta in order to test bathymetric variants within a GIS framework. The project is now entering an operational phase in which local actors are using this method, together with developers, in the field.

Digital replication has now become a trivial operation; its importance lies in the fact that the structures derived from these models can be repeatedly subjected to simulations that produce a broad array of comparative scenarios. The real question, therefore, is the designer's ability to frame reality within a model that can mimic a situation and be tested relative to specific simulation goals. This heuristic approach using models to sketch, test, and compare conceptual ideas in three dimensions, as in the case of the Ciliwung River, opens prospects that were hitherto inaccessible or difficult and time-consuming to explore. Digital modeling has enhanced, and in part replaced, the role of two-dimensional paper sketching and mapping; it can now be used to test and heighten–in three, and sometimes four, dimensions–various physical aspects of a project in the making. In this sense, the descriptive models used by landscape architects and the predictive models used by engineers are conflated into an instrument for shaping plausible new realities (following pages).

When we deal with modeling, the actual framing, selecting, and processing of an ever-growing quantity of data is of primary interest to us. Modeling increases both the scope and substance of an analysis, delivering (sometimes serendipitously) the most unexpected and fruitful results. The use of terrestrial laser scanners and photogrammetric instruments, such as drones at the Landscape Visualization and Modeling Lab (LVML), has enabled the gathering of considerable amounts of information about an existing site to an unprecedented

## Visualization of Flood Results - (Normal Flow)

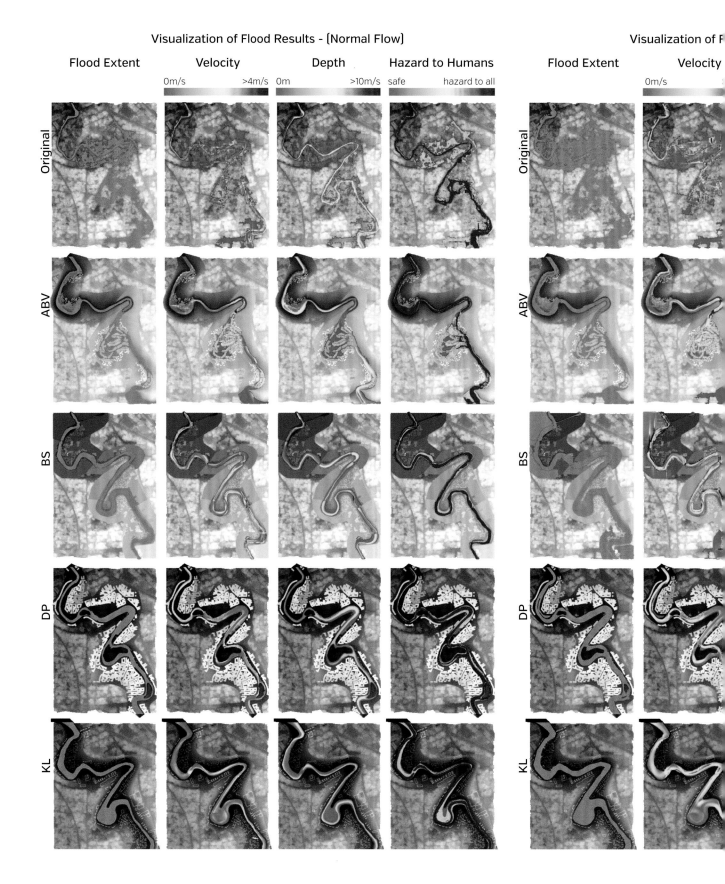

Visualization of F

Flood Extent   Velocity   Depth   Hazard to Humans

0m/s   >4m/s   0m   >10m/s   safe   hazard to all

Flood Extent   Velocity

0m/s

Original

ABV

BS

DP

KL

ts - [Minor Flow]

## Visualization of Flood Results - [Major Flow]

| Depth | Hazard to Humans | Flood Extent | Velocity | Depth | Hazard to Humans |
|---|---|---|---|---|---|

>10m/s    safe    hazard to all      0m/s    >4m/s    0m    >10m/s    safe    hazard to all

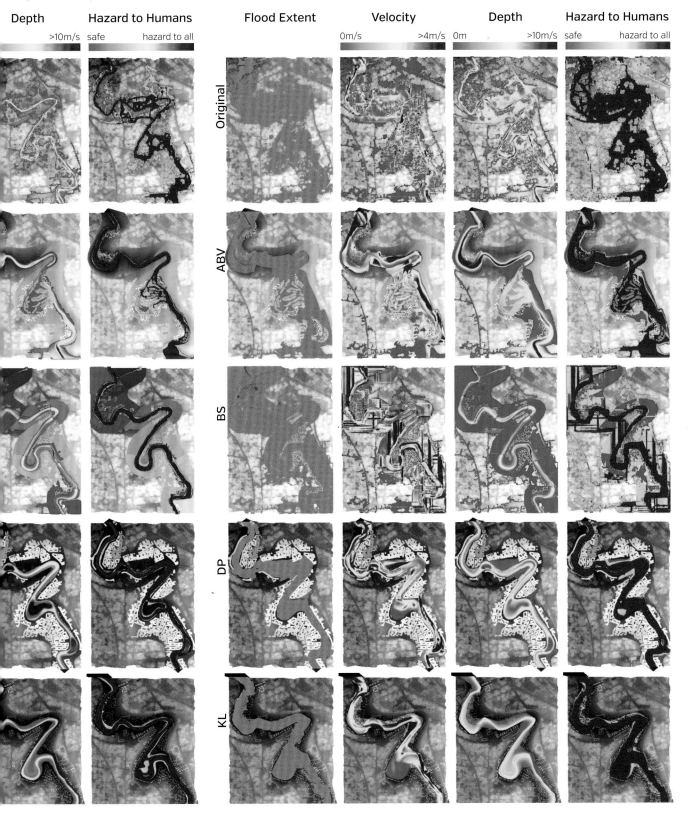

degree of accuracy. The digital landscape models derived from this technology come within a few centimeters of reality in all three x, y, and z axes. Yet their representation of reality remains extremely reductive and partial. In his *Scientific Autobiography*, Aldo Rossi recalls how architecture students repeatedly measured a small Renaissance piazza by hand, each time coming up with slightly different results.[3] The piazza formed a trapezoid on a slope, and it was actually impossible to fix and verify definitively both the measurements and the actual urban space being drawn: it was all about the art of infinite approximation. This is a beautiful allegory of how we tend asymptotically toward representing reality through sharper descriptive models, without ever actually attaining a fully precise representation. Mimesis should be understood not so much in absolute terms, but rather in terms of the tools and topological expectations that we set for ourselves within a given project frame.

As with any form of representation, mimesis through digital simulation will always remain a false show of sorts, far removed from the true depth, scope, and physical substance of landscape in its entirety. The more a landscape imitation may claim to be real, the more fraudulent it becomes. To quote Alfred Korzybski's famous dictum, "The map is not the territory." So how do we imbue our models and simulations with immanent meaning and suitable accuracy to remain believable? Firstly, understanding the genius of place is a subjective thing that cannot be fully replicated by any form of representation, analog or digital. Countless facets of a given landscape cannot be communicated through a model; rather, the model is an intentional reduction of reality. The modeling tool plays a critical role in extending one's experience of a site through specific framing and mimesis, revealing entirely new readings of a site. The goal is to project the design vision of possible futures for any given site. The instruments of topology simply extend our professional expertise, like tools of visualization in the medical sector. True to its inherent definition, virtual simulation creates a break with the genuine plasticity of a landscape. It is a form of abstraction, calling on our senses in a contained and limited way; it is meant to control appearances and to frame a set of selective visions with intent and purpose. In fact, mimesis relies on the viewer's interpretation of the model and its association with the authentic object, as happens with a perspective drawing or collage.[4]

In the case of a project by the Atelier Girot at the Domaine de Montplaisir in southern France, the topographic model, which was based on the interpolation of point cloud data generated by drones, is reduced to a black-and-white abstract topology with great terrain accuracy. The landscape simulations underwent a strong formal reduction for the sake of clarity and to better communicate the object of study. At an initial design stage, the model of this historic estate reveals a series of spatial and scenographic opportunities. The initial point cloud model generated by a terrestrial laser scanner represents a complex terrain with significant flooding problems. Simplified to a digital skin of dots wrapped around the volumetric boundary of the site under observation, the model becomes an important tool to convey information. It can be further utilized to simulate such processes as water flow or temperature flow, with the particles colorized depending on flow velocity and direction. This helps the designer to identify areas prone to erosion, in the case of water, or heat traps, in the case of air flow. Both issues are of prime importance in this Mediterranean region, which is prone to heat waves and flash floods. Quantifiable information in a point cloud model hence articulates an objective description and can anticipate varying environmental conditions. In this case, simulation is a substitute for experimenting directly on the terrain; it is, therefore, not a substitute for reality but a very useful complement to an ongoing design process. Simulation, in this instance, has to do with an art of terrain replication showing structural complexity through differentiated surface textures, which can be of great interest at both historic and archeological sites where the goal is to preserve the ground topography intact. Thanks to advances in computing power, as well sensor and software developments, increased data accuracy in landscape

Previous page: Flood simulation of four different bathymetric design models for the Kampung Melayu neighborhood, with the reference model on top. Here, the descriptive (designed) models are also used as predictive models to run various flood events through a series of computer simulations with widely varying results.

Opposite: Plan view of a point cloud model of the Zimmermann Garden in Brissago.

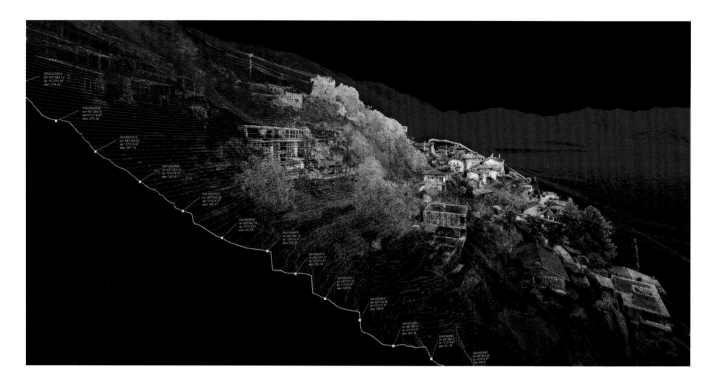

architecture modeling can now contribute to the elaboration of a project across a broad range of scales, from specific construction details to the most experimental techniques in spatial and temporal modeling of terrain.

Simulations are highly manipulative and can be applied to a broad range of aspects of landscape architecture. Through digital simulation, the landscape can be decomposed into specific modes of representation with various degrees of abstraction as a means to show particular aspects of a place. While the data's generative potential can help to optimize solutions, an intervention can also deliberately disrupt the status quo and impose an entirely new logic. For example, mountain lakes in the Swiss Alps are often the result of landslides. The sudden change jumbles the order of flora and fauna, sometimes impacting the larger system with positive or negative consequences. The same can happen with the construction of manmade structures, such as dams, roads, or any other earthwork, and this is where simulations play an essential role in substantiating the impact of a new transformation. Research at the ETH Future Cities Laboratory has shown that point cloud models help to push the limits of design to much larger territorial scales; for example, simulating the impact of dams on flood events in three dimensions at the scale of an entire valley.[5] Simulation is thus a powerful tool of investigation, not in terms of photorealistic rendering but in its capacity to verify what happens to a landscape through changing ambient conditions. This physical apprehension of a site, as a body to be dissected and analyzed, entirely changes the approach to landscape design. Landscape architects once relied exclusively on mapping and approximate models

to generate their designs; now we can use extremely precise datasets to test hypotheses and develop future scenarios.

The Zimmerman Garden project in Brissago by Atelier Girot overlooks Lago Maggiore from Switzerland. The use of a point cloud model has proved crucial. The existing 18th-century terraces are poorly mapped and the slopes are extremely steep and difficult to work with. The terrain sections and views produced from the point cloud model were very useful throughout the entire design and construction detailing process. The advantage of the simulation was its incredible topographic accuracy. Simulation can also be understood as a point of departure from mapping, and the precision with which the terrain is depicted allows the designer to 'physically' cross-check design options that were previously mapped out on paper. The modeling is operative and enables the designer to test options before they go any further.

Simulation can also be used at the other end of the design spectrum in virtual fabrication and communication. The point cloud based model has been developed at the LVML as a very powerful tool of representation that can generate both stills and animated simulations. The role of such simulations is no longer analytical or forensic, but helps to test future scenarios. Digital landscape simulation has become a potent means to help develop design concepts in the early stages of a project. And while it offers a powerful tool of analysis and design, the point cloud model's diaphanous structure made of light and mass simultaneously constitutes a break from the original idea of place while reviving a different kind of gaze in situ. Such was the challenge encountered in the ETH research project of the

Klybeck Island in Basel that required the complex embedding of a waterfront proposal in the existing physical context of the old harbor and its river.[6] The virtual insertion of the designed model into a point cloud base, which itself became the basis of a video-tracking project, helped to frame the project in a strongly suggestive simulated context. It brought tangible proof of a potentially strong landscape and even helped raise polemic questions about the future of the Basel Harbor. Here again the question of aesthetics and the degree of abstraction and amount of detail needed for a strong video simulation play a major role in the way it is communicated and received.

In the examples discussed above, the goal of simulation is to investigate and communicate the anticipated impact of potential designs at a given site. Using feedback loops, simulations bridge the realm of the exact site model with that of the designer's vision by showing various facets of a project, understanding design as something always in progress and subject to change. Landscape designs commonly span metric scales of 1:2000 to 1:20, comprising the realms of planning and architectural design. Simulations need to work accordingly, increasing or decreasing in detail depending on the scale in order to reach the critical point of interest while withholding any obsolete or superfluous information. Each form of abstraction, therefore, frames a response at a specific scale taken from the real world. Simulation projects the viewer into a familiar spatial environment, revealed as abstracted form, and it unfolds quite differently from reality while remaining analogous to it.

The difference between traditional methods of design that use orthographic projection, and three-dimensional point cloud modeling lies in the great versatility of the tool, which allows the designer to operate across scales and maneuver seamlessly from a detailed view of a place back to the overall scope of a site. This understanding of simulation is quite different from Korzybski's notion suggesting a radical distinction between models of reality and reality itself. The use of simulation in landscape architecture does not necessarily rely on the faithfulness of its depiction of the real world, but rather on a three-dimensional abstraction tied to precise geographic parameters on which new content can be tested, manipulated, and superimposed. The importance of the new art of point cloud simulation is not that it brings us closer to some perfect representation of our world, but that it enables us to frame a simulation knowingly within a strong landscape vision, one capable of facing an increasingly challenging reality to come.

1 Plato, *The Republic*, trans. Allan Bloom (New York: Harper and Collins, 1991).

2 Theodor Adorno, *Aesthetic Theory* (London: Routledge and Kegan Paul, 1984).

3 Aldo Rossi, *A Scientific Autobiography* (Chicago: Graham Foundation; New York, Institute for Architecture and Urban Studies, 1981).

4 Jean Baudrillard, *Simulacra and Simulation* (Ann Arbor: University of Michigan Press, 1994).

5 Ervine Lin, et. al., "Developing River Rehabilitation Scenarios by Integrating Landscape and Hydrodynamic Modeling For The Ciliwung River in Jakarta Indonesia," *Sustainable Cities and Society* 20 (January 2016): 180–98.

6 The goal of the research project developed at the Landscape Visualization and Modeling Lab (LVML) at the Swiss Federal Institute of Technology (ETH) in Zürich was to uncover a new landscape potential for the Klybeck Island in Basel, Switzerland by transforming the former island into an inviting large public area for the city.

Opposite: A section through the point cloud model of the Zimmermann Garden in Brissago.

# EDUARDO RICO + ENRIQUETA LLABRES VALLS
# INTERACTING WITH SIMULATIONS

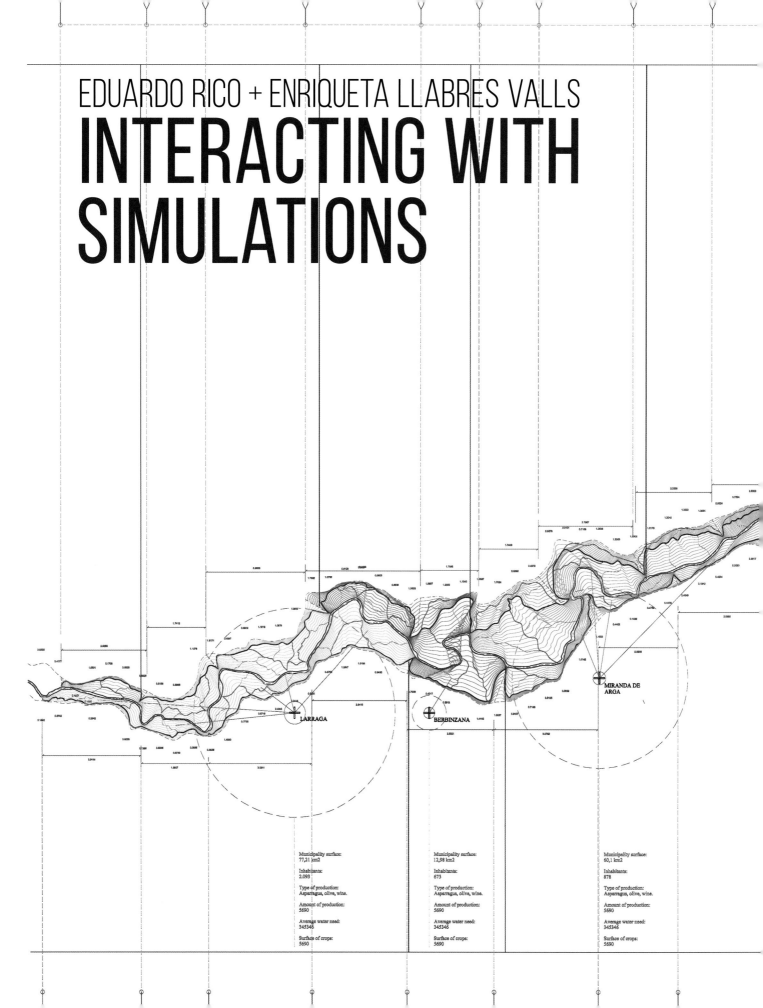

LARRAGA

BERBINZANA

MIRANDA DE ARGA

Municipality surface:
77,21 km2

Inhabitants:
2.093

Type of production:
Asparragus, olive, wine.

Amount of production:
5690

Average water need:
345346

Surface of crops:
5690

Municipality surface:
12,98 km2

Inhabitants:
673

Type of production:
Asparragus, olive, wine.

Amount of production:
5690

Average water need:
345346

Surface of crops:
5690

Municipality surface:
60,1 km2

Inhabitants:
878

Type of production:
Asparragus, olive, wine.

Amount of production:
5690

Average water need:
345346

Surface of crops:
5690

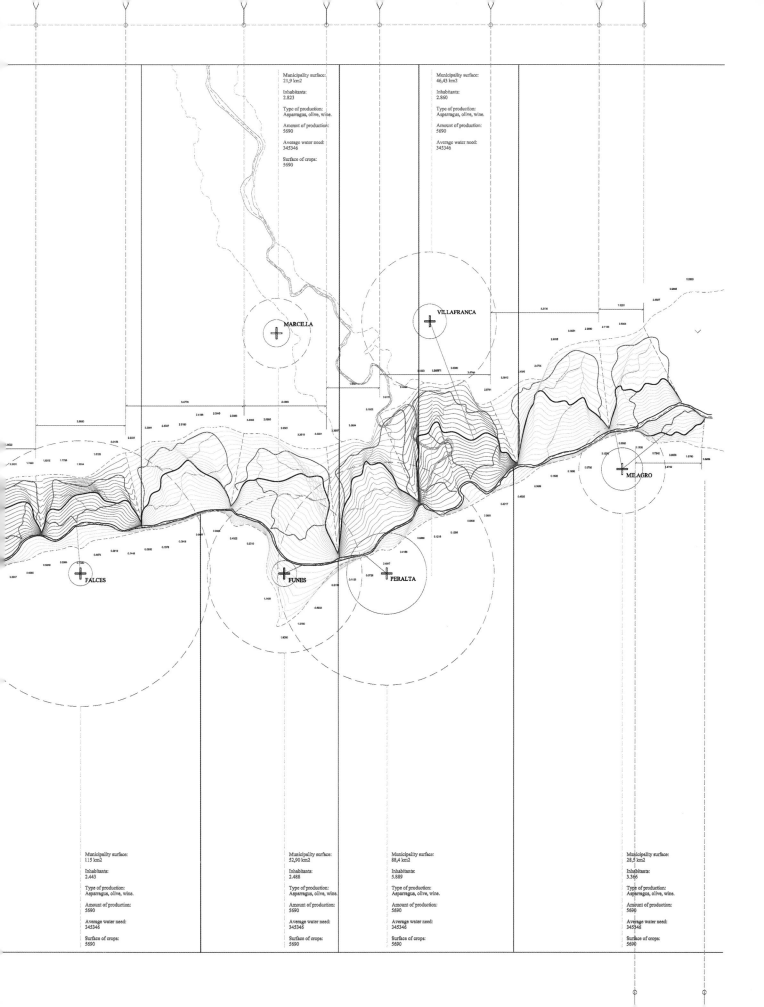

MARCILLA

VILLAFRANCA

MILAGRO

FALCES

FUNES

PERALTA

Municipality surface:
21,9 km2

Inhabitants:
2.823

Type of production:
Asparragus, olive, wine.

Amount of production:
5690

Average water need:
345346

Surface of crops:
5690

Municipality surface:
46,43 km2

Inhabitants:
2.860

Type of production:
Asparragus, olive, wine.

Amount of production:
5690

Average water need:
345346

Municipality surface:
115 km2

Inhabitants:
2.443

Type of production:
Asparragus, olive, wine.

Amount of production:
5690

Average water need:
345346

Surface of crops:
5690

Municipality surface:
52,90 km2

Inhabitants:
2.488

Type of production:
Asparragus, olive, wine.

Amount of production:
5690

Average water need:
345346

Surface of crops:
5690

Municipality surface:
88,4 km2

Inhabitants:
5.889

Type of production:
Asparragus, olive, wine.

Amount of production:
5690

Average water need:
345346

Surface of crops:
5690

Municipality surface:
28,5 km2

Inhabitants:
3.366

Type of production:
Asparragus, olive, wine.

Amount of production:
5690

Average water need:
345346

Surface of crops:
5690

Eduardo Rico is a civil engineer and graduate of the AA's landscape urbanism program. He is co-director of the office Relational Urbanism. He is currently engaged in strategic advice on infrastructure and transportation for urban master planning projects at Arup. Rico's work and research focus on alternative design practices that feed infrastructural inputs into architectural urbanism. Rico is a visiting Lecturer in Landscape Architecture at Harvard Graduate School of Design, teaches at The Bartlett, and is currently co-director of the MArch and MSc Landscape Urbanism programs at the Architectural Association.

Enriqueta Llabres Valls is an architect from Barcelona with a masters in Local Economic Development from The London School of Economics. She is currently a visiting Lecturer in Landscape Architecture at Harvard Graduate School of Design and director of a research cluster at The Bartlett, UCL. Together with Eduardo Rico, Valls established Relational Urbanism, a multidisciplinary architecture office in London, and directed the Relational Urbanism Design Studio at the Berlage Institute between 2011 and 2013.

➕ ENGINEERING, HYDROLOGY, ARCHITECTURE

In October 2000 in Florence, the members of the Council of Europe signed the European Landscape Convention, with the aim of promoting "the protection, management and planning of landscape in Europe, and to organize European co-operation."[1] The first point of this convention defines landscape as "an area, as perceived by people, whose character is the result of the action and interaction of natural and/or human factors."[2] The use of the word perceived in this definition implies that landscape is not just constructed in the physical sense (i.e., literally built through human interaction with material reality) but is a way of seeing, which is also constructed (in this case discursively) and far from natural or simply given to us. As Denis Cosgrove would argue, we need to be aware of this double layering of the 'constructedness' of landscape, asking ourselves how we choose to describe what we do, what are the conventions behind these forms of representation, and what are the ideological consequences of these choices.[3]

The advent of digital technologies as applied to territorial practices has enabled a vast array of new forms of representation, some of which go beyond graphic description of the environment and emphasize our capacity to interact with dynamic systems, often in real time. Digital interfaces, computer-based simulations of dynamic landscapes, and performance analysis through GIS are all techniques that open up new avenues and even new disciplinary approaches, helping us to create this 'second level' of a landscape's construction.

In this context, designers cannot remain in the comfort zone created by these techniques, using them purely as data sources for technically sound proposals backed up by scientific evidence. On the contrary, they need to move on and ask themselves: what are the critical potentials associated with these forms of representation? The designer's task, it could be argued, is to derive alternative regimes of effect (using the same abstractions that substantiate these tools) in order to seek new forms of spatial production and to constantly assess them against the existing discourses of territorial disciplines.[4] What follows is an attempt to elucidate the potentials that simulation techniques offer for a new form of territorial praxis by highlighting the nature of these simulations and paying special attention to the ways in which users can interact with them.

The use of simulations at landscape and territorial scales has a longstanding tradition within the earth sciences, and it is precisely the interplay between the digital and the material world that makes them so relevant for designers today. As early as the mid-19th century, physical scale models of geological processes were built to interpret the complex patterns of material distribution across the earth's surface.[5] Developments in hydraulics and aerodynamics were similarly accompanied by the use of physical models to simulate large-scale processes, initially for explanatory emphasis (i.e., to understand complex phenomena in a qualitative way), but later as a form of prediction and accurate measurement. This shift toward prediction and assessment was made possible by the theory of Dimensional Analysis, developed at the end of the 19th century, which helps designers understand how measurements in a small-scale model relate to their real counterparts. Equally important, Dimensional Analysis tells us that the limits of the model's applicability are due to small-scale material effects that can mask the results of interest. This has two main consequences: on one hand, a model can be scaled down only so far before it stops being representative of the process being modeled; on the other hand, materials with suitable properties (density, grain size) necessary to comply with the mathematics of the scaled-down version may simply not exist, or may be very difficult to obtain.

In contrast, digital simulations can address any territorial process without the problems of material scale associated with physical models and can offer easier

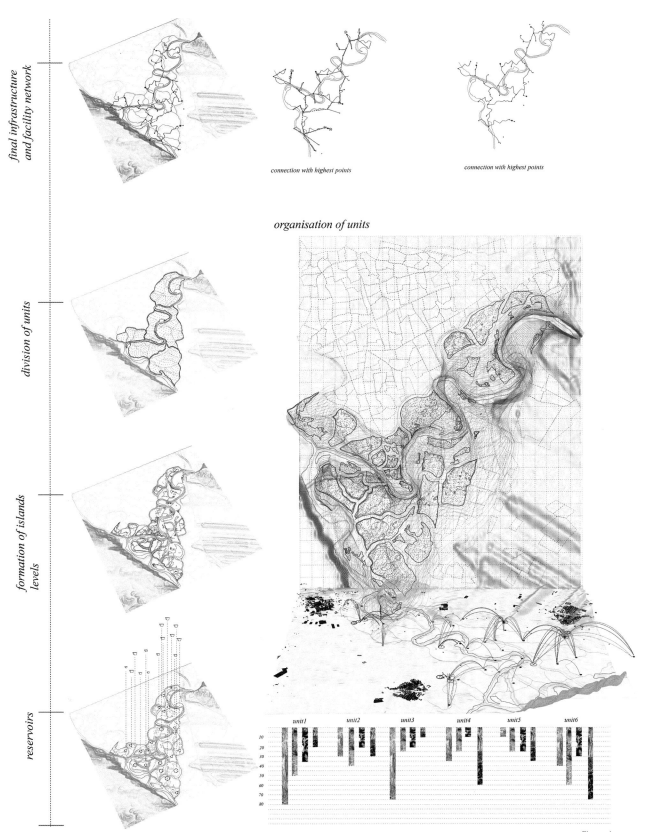

final infrastructure
and facility network

connection with highest points

connection with highest points

organisation of units

division of units

formation of islands
levels

reservoirs

unit1  unit2  unit3  unit4  unit5  unit6

Figure 1

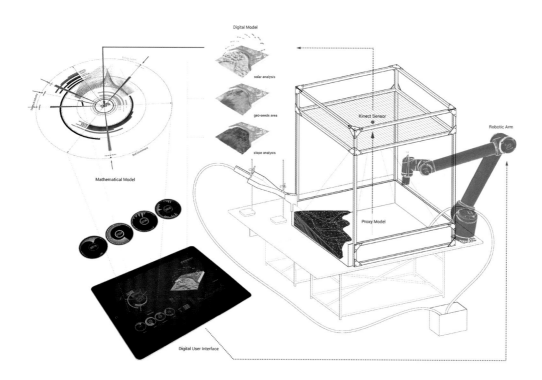

Figure 2: Development of user interfaces (proposed with robot arm end effector) showcase real-time analysis of formed topography alongside ecological modeling.

access to data and analysis. These models, developed during the second half of the 20th century, have gained prevalence over physical models thanks to the increased availability of computer power.[6] The main problem with digital simulations, though, is that it is difficult to initially assess whether the model contains all relevant levels of the complex behaviors being modeled, or if it is missing second-order effects that are not initially built into its mathematics.

This is where the 'live' quality of material simulations plays an important role, since their continuous real-time evolution allows the user to assess what is happening and make a value judgment about the model's completeness. This aspect of time evolution in physical models adds a qualitative dimension to the understanding of processes, making them still a valuable tool in analysis. Along these lines, physical models are commonly used to calibrate and corroborate digital models, which can be easily adapted to various conditions after the user has 'seen' them working in the first place.

Designers have much to learn from this dual method of working with models. While the purpose of simulations in landscape or architectural design is not necessarily the development of purely analytical and contrastable information, the use of these tools can discover ideas about processes, change, and ultimately material transformations of a territory caused by human or natural forces. This article argues for a combination of both digital and physical modeling as a means to achieve new forms of design agency and engagement with both the designer and the public. It

will do so by describing several projects where different types of simulations have proved to be instrumental at various design stages and for various audiences.

In the first example, students from the AA Landscape Urbanism program used context-specific simulations to analyze large portions of a territory, looking for ways to reconfigure these territories using natural processes.[7] The project sought to discover possible alternative forms of river management in the agricultural economies of La Rioja, Spain, based on alterations of the existing river flow. It borrowed ideas from current proposals in various parts of Europe where rivers are allowed to behave naturally in certain sections in order to alleviate flooding elsewhere. Projects such as Room for the River in the Netherlands, and frameworks such as the River Restoration Project in the UK both stress the environmental and flood-control benefits of these approaches, which are currently being applied and monitored extensively.[8] The students' proposal emphasizes the need to incorporate agricultural activities and spatial design, using the tendency of rivers to generate alternative routes for water to flow through. These routes can in turn yield plot division systems that can enhance local production, and also tend to improve the ecological value of the riverbed by increasing the overall length of the shoreline and generating diverse shoreline conditions.

A river flow simulation was used to study the exiting flows of Spain's Arga River. Students analyzed potential scenarios for the branching out of the main channel, in most cases by utilizing abandoned channels or creating new routes for the water (Figure 1). The model was based on a cellular automata abstraction of the terrain that was composed of a grid of cells, each of which contained a column of soil and water.[9] The tendency of each cell to erode or capture sediment depends on the water's speed as well as its sediment load. Inputs for the model are topography and soil conditions obtained from GIS and data on water flows, including the frequency and severity of flood events. The model then simulates a number of flood events within the riverbed, each of which causes changes in the structure of the floodplain. The result is an evolutionary version of the landscape, which helps to predict the river's tendency to move laterally.

The students used the model to discover weak points in the river banks and divide the wider floodplain into separate 'free' zones or segments where the river is allowed to migrate safely over time, following its natural tendency in what are called anastomosing channels (p.58–9). These sections are further developed as new forms of productive patterns linked to collective forms of agriculture, according to their location in relation to existing population. The project proposes the possibility of river management based on the river's local behavior and linked to forms of governance that correspond to the newly formed anastomosing sections. The digital simulations enabled a detailed study of a given context, unveiling the river's potential to reconfigure the landscape and the administrative regimes of the agricultural economy.

In the second example, also from AA Landscape Urbanism, a digital simulation was used in order to address the detailed design of prototypes that can capture sediments in an evolutionary way. The students looked at the dynamics of sand movement at the mouth of the Nile River, in the Demietta Sand Ribbon near Lake Manzala.[10] The sediment load from the river is transported eastward by the oblique incidence of waves, generating sand spits that grow over time and form further layers of the existing lake, which is extensively used for fish farming. Sand extraction from the nearby Suez Canal can be utilized to facilitate further expansion of adjacent fisheries, thereby addressing food shortages in Egypt but also opening up new political issues of sediment distribution and geomorphological agency along the Mediterranean coast.

The students used a simulation to generate a prototype for a series of controlled spits where local insertions of sediments cause the sand to accumulate in a semi-predictable manner. The process of spit formation can be modeled through a cellular automata simulation that begins with an initial lake shoreline in which sediment moves from one cell to another depending on the surrounding lake level and the influence of a site-specific wave population.[11] The model can produce animations that help to elucidate the movement of sediments along a dynamic shoreline; it can also be interrupted at any time, modified, and easily reintroduced into the code for a new run.

This time-based aspect of the model—its capacity to accept feedback—was crucial in the generation of detailed forms of 'capturing' sediment, allowing the designer to insert interventions and continue running the model to see how the sand bar would close to form lagoons. These lagoons could later become part of the fish farm economy of Lake Manzala, creating a link between a crafted form of geomorphology and the social structures operating on the site. In comparison to the first example, the model used in this project was harder to insert into the local context (as adapting existing bathymetry to the code was time-consuming and not always effective). However, this second model was also easier to interact with, making it more appropriate as a tool for generative design proposals.

In a third case, a physical model not only helps the designer to understand complex dynamics, but can also be used to engage an external audience. It shows the work carried out in the RC18 research cluster, part of the Bartlett Urban Morphogenesis Lab, which engages with the process of regeneration of tailings arising from tar sand extraction in Alberta, Canada.[12] The students' work examined the tailings' formation process and speculated on the possibility of mobilizing them toward alternative forms of landscape.

Sediment extracted as part of the oil mining process is mixed with water and left to settle in large open-air ponds called tailing ponds. The type of formation produced in these ponds is similar to those in Gilbert deltas, which are typical where rivers enter large inland bodies of water. Gilbert deltas can be simulated in a laboratory tank as water and sediments flow from a high point in the tank and arrive at a static, ponded volume of water that remains at a constant level. Data for these models can be gathered via laser reading (with a one-millimeter degree of accuracy in assessing the water level) or through image reading of color-coded materials. Once digitized, the model is linked to an ecological model that can analyze and represent the population dynamics of species in the newly generated landscape (Figure 2).

This simulation has a short response time, which would enable the user to trace the effects of sediment and water as the channels migrate over the surface of the delta, generating islands and abandoned arms of the river. Action and reaction can be experienced in real time so that the model user can understand the consequences of introducing alien bodies, walls, or other forms of obstruction (Figure 3). The students used this feature to develop a system of terraces that diverted the flow of sediments as these were dropped into the tailing pond.

This last project went on to encompass the generation of an interactive environment where members of the public could engage with the physical and digital realm simultaneously. The students proposed an installation in which the small-scale

1 Council of Europe, "The European Landscape Convention," http://www.coe.int/en/web/landscape/-/8th-council-of-europe-conference-on-the-implementation-of-the-european-landscape-convention- (accessed August 5, 2015).

2 Council of Europe, "Details of Treaty No. 176," http://conventions.coe.int/Treaty/en/Treaties/Html/176.htm (accessed August 5, 2015).

3 Denis E. Cosgrove, "The Idea of Landscape," in *Social Formation and Symbolic Landscape*, (Madison: University of Wisconsin Press, 1984), 13-38.

4 For an extended discussion on the role of diagrammatic representation in landscape, urban, and territorial praxis see D. Spencer, "Landscape Urbanism, Praxis and the Spatial Turn" in *Landscape Sensitive Design* (Trento: LIStLab, 2010), 20.

5 Angela N. H. Creager, Elizabeth Lunbeck, & M. Norton Wise, *Science without Laws: Model Systems, Cases, Exemplary Narratives* (Durham, NC: Duke University Press, 2007).

6 Ibid.

7 Silvia Ribot, Dimitra Bra & Lida Driva, "Anastomosing River Project," AA Landscape Urbanism. Co-directed by Eduardo Rico & Alfredo Ramirez. Design tutor: Clara Oloriz. Course seminars: Tom Smith & Douglas Spencer.

8 "Room for the River," https://www.ruimtevoorderivier.nl/english/ (accessed August 5, 2015); River Restoration Centre website, http://www.therrc.co.uk/ (accessed August 5, 2015).

9 Details of the model can be found in Tom Coulthard, "The Cellular Automaton Evolutionary Slope and River Model (CAESAR)," University of Hull, http://www.coulthard.org.uk/downloads/CAESAR_instructions2.pdf (accessed August 5, 2015).

10 Ting Fu Chang, Liam Mouritz, & Xiabin Hu, "Littoral Negotiations Project," AA Landscape Urbanism. Co-directed by Eduardo Rico & Alfredo Ramirez. Design tutor: Clara Oloriz. Course seminars: Tom Smith & Douglas Spencer.

11 Model scripted in Python by the design team based on the Coastline Evolution Model, initially developed by A. Brad Murray of Duke University (http://csdms.colorado.edu/wiki/Model:CEM) and further developed by Andy Barkwirth of Nottingham University (http://www.bgs.ac.uk/staff/profiles/25120.html, accessed August 5, 2015).

12 Jiateng Sun, et al., "[Re]Tailing City Project," Bartlett BPRo, UDII, Research Cluster 18. Tutors: Eduardo Rico, Enriqueta Llabres, & Zachary Fluker. Lab Leader: Claudia Pasquero.

river model is captured live and a digital model is projected alongside it (Figure 2). This quality of interaction is possible due to the speed at which the model reacts to change and water flow, which, in this case, would be appreciable within two minutes of the introduction of changes in the physical medium. Of the various models discussed in this essay, this one is perhaps the least rigorous from an analytical perspective, since small-scale effects do not have an accurate dimensional relationship to real effects. On the other hand, the physical quality of the model and the fact that it responds in real time to playful manipulations by users provides a new tacit dimension, allowing people to discover interdependencies between physical and environmental effects in ways that a single drawing cannot display. In this context, the term 'tacit' refers to Michael Polanyi's definition of a type of knowledge that can be transmitted even though it cannot be systematically codified, linking the work to types of knowledge typically found in the arts or creative industries.

The examples presented here point to different scales and forms of design agency that are made possible by the digital and physical simulation of landscape formations. A comparison among the model types suggests a certain tradeoff between accuracy and interactivity in such a way that simulation tools can be targeted to different audiences depending on the designer's agenda. As in more analytic disciplines, where physical and digital simulations are used in a complementary way, designers can benefit from both types of work. Simulations that may be more sketchy or imprecise (such as the third case and, to a lesser extent, the second one) may result in a more intuitive interaction with the user, opening up the potential for forms of tacit knowledge to enter the project. On the other hand, more precise and context-aware simulations (as in the first case described here) may point to hidden traces and locally specific clues that can be used to define integral parts of the design. The designer's task is to be aware of what forms of knowledge are prompted by these tools and to think of ways of inserting them into the project in order to advance a more critically aware territorial praxis.

7

8

10

11

12

13

14 Mesh

2:00   4:00   6:00   8:00   10:00   12:00   14:00

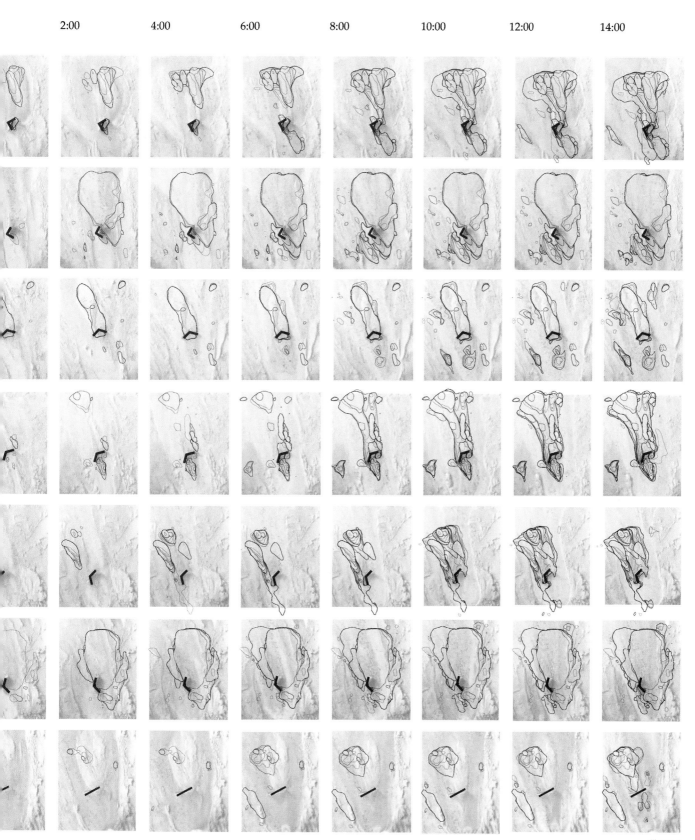

Figure 3

# KAREN M'CLOSKEY + KEITH VANDERSYS
# TESTING THE WATERS

Karen M'Closkey + Keith VanDerSys are founding partners of PEG office of landscape + architecture and faculty in the department of landscape architecture at the University of Pennsylvania. Their recent work explores advances in environmental modeling and simulation tools. They are authors of *Dynamic Patterns: Visualizing Landscapes in a Digital Age* (2016).

**+** COMPUTATION, HYDROLOGY

Advancements in computation enable designers to engage the temporal and relational qualities inherent to the medium of landscape. This project, located along the Delaware River in Philadelphia, explores wetland suitability strategies that are guided by *energy* and *elevation* parameters visualized through geospatial analysis (GIS), computational flow dynamics (Aquaveo SRH-2D), and parametric software (Grasshopper).

Two key challenges exist when integrating hydrodynamic simulation into design methods: reliable data and software interoperability. First, waterway data are mapped mainly for navigational purposes and are often too coarse, out-of-date, or even absent for the purposes of design. A combination of topographic and bathymetric geospatial data (available through PASDA, NOAA, and USACE) show that shoreline information is missing. These data gaps are characteristic of many rivers, which leave data collection up to designers. For example, data for this project were gathered by attaching a GPS /depth-finder to a remote-controlled fish-bait boat.

Second, data transfer among the various software platforms remains difficult, yet is needed to create a hydrodynamic model. The translation of data among analytic, simulation, and design environments requires custom scripts. Designers must be active tool 'makers' not simply tool users. Data can then be examined to see the differential water velocities and directions under a variety of flow volumes and tidal heights. In this project, these variabilities are used to determine wetland creation suitability. Successive design interventions can be run through the simulation in order to understand how flow responds to alterations in profile, depth, and material. This process uses numerically and metrically precise information yet fosters the iterative testing of many design scenarios within the model.

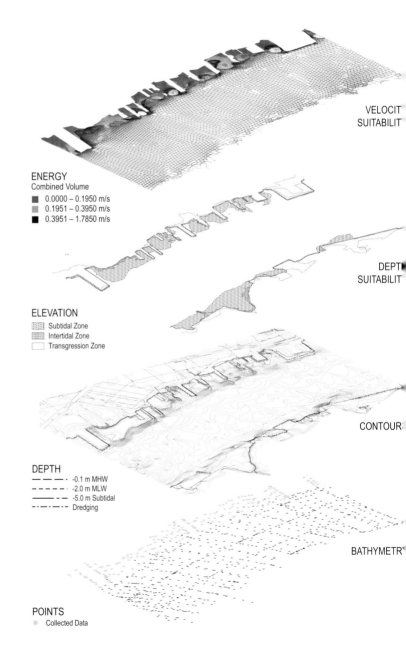

VELOCIT
SUITABILIT

**ENERGY**
Combined Volume
- ▓ 0.0000 – 0.1950 m/s
- ▒ 0.1951 – 0.3950 m/s
- ■ 0.3951 – 1.7850 m/s

DEPT
SUITABILIT

**ELEVATION**
- ▦ Subtidal Zone
- ▦ Intertidal Zone
- ☐ Transgression Zone

CONTOUR

**DEPTH**
- – – – -0.1 m MHW
- - - - - -2.0 m MLW
- ——— -5.0 m Subtidal
- ·–·–·– Dredging

BATHYMETR

**POINTS**
- ● Collected Data

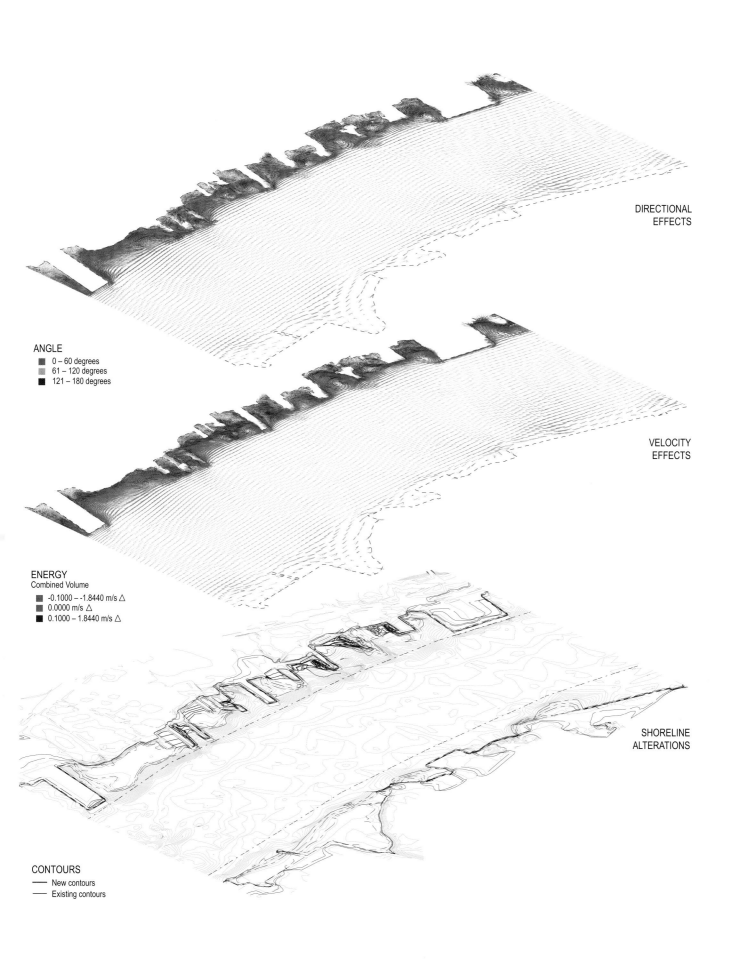

DIRECTIONAL
EFFECTS

VELOCITY
EFFECTS

SHORELINE
ALTERATIONS

# BRADLEY CANTRELL
# ADAPTATION

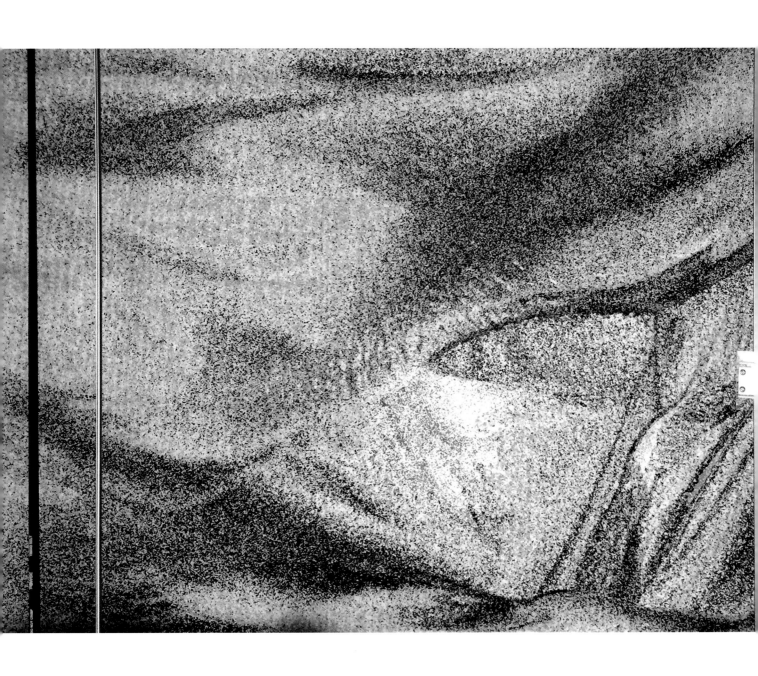

Bradley Cantrell is an Associate Professor of Landscape Architectural Technology at Harvard University. His research focuses on the role of computation in environmental and ecological design looking at infrastructures and devices that create complex interrelationships among maintenance, evolved processes, and environmental response. His book, *Responsive Landscapes* (2016), co-authored with Justine Holzman, looks at architecture, landscape architecture, computer science, and art that employ technologies as mediators of landscape processes.

✚ HYDROLOGY, ENGINEERING

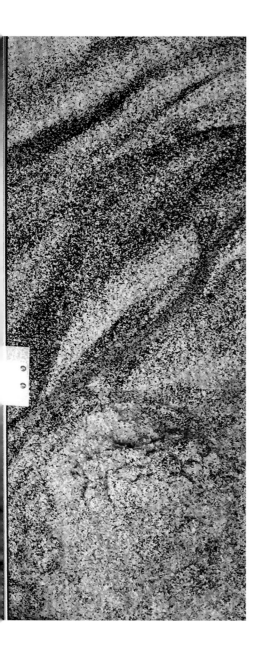

Responsive technologies is a general term for devices or components that enable methods of sensing, monitoring, processing, and feedback. For example, the F-35 Joint Strike Fighter Jet currently being developed by Lockheed Martin is a sensory platform that provides pilots with on-board radar, weapons guidance, navigation, and environmental mediation. The F-35's pilot, while not physically manipulating the aircraft's flaps and rudders, can apply a range of technologies to travel faster than the speed of sound or deliver ordnance from miles away to targets in the air or on the ground with sub-millimeter precision.[1] The platform not only creates new forms of vision, hearing, and feeling but also allows the pilot to make small adjustments to controls that affect the plane's mechanical and hydraulic systems. The feedback loop between human, machine, and environment in the F-35 occurs in real time and requires thousands of interpretations of environmental conditions to provide accurate feedback to the pilot. The interpreted environment makes possible sophisticated interactions between the pilot controlling the aircraft and the plane's flight.

The F-35 is an extreme case, but we see similar versions of this relationship in the implementation of responsive technologies in commercial agriculture, transportation logistics, consumer electronic devices, and a host of other applications. The automatic door opener at the grocery store, the Nest thermostat in a house, and the Roomba domestic vacuum are all familiar forms of responsive technologies. For the purpose of projecting future conditions, it is worthwhile to speculate on an ecological or infrastructural equivalent to the F-35: a highly symbiotic connection between the constructed and the biologic, enabled by real-time simulations that drive responsive technologies. This symbiosis draws on the inherent uncertainty of hydraulic models but reacts precisely through small modifications that are evaluated and applied to evolve future feedback. The uncertainty of these models spawns from the modeler's construction of an alternate reality that abstracts complex fluid systems through averaging, random value generation, and minimization of variables for computational efficiency.

Nascent efforts across multiple disciplines are engaging ecological systems with forms of real-time simulation and responsive technologies.[2] These efforts range from drone seed dispersal to autonomous terrain grading to in situ genetic manipulation of biological systems. Each of these efforts alters the current paradigm of design, evaluation, and construction and offers entry points for an adaptive method of ecological manipulation. Because hydrologic systems are in a constant state of flux, there are ongoing attempts by designers to develop methodologies that explore the creation of adaptive landscapes that engage responsive technologies and ecological systems. Responsive technologies enable a degree of adaptive control that directly addresses the indeterminacy inherent in landscapes and their ongoing processes of change. When we consider how these mechanisms of adaptive control might

be embedded in our landscapes in the future, various questions emerge. What role do models and simulation have in the design of new forms of infrastructure and ecological systems? What is the relationship between the simulation and the physical environment? How might we leverage the potential of simulation, analysis, and visualization tools to advance an ecological system's ability to adaptively synthesize biotic and abiotic systems?

The implementation of responsive technologies requires frameworks that not only engage landscapes at the site scale but also acknowledge the territory and interconnections of ecological systems. These frameworks are not imagined as overarching methods of control but instead express a relationship between sensing and processing that is predicated on learning and that activates natural processes such as succession, accretion, and remediation as agents of change in the environment. This method privileges the dynamics of ecology over static constructions as a method by which to design landscape systems. Within responsive technologies reside programmed interactions driven by logics, the instructions that define how the systems process sensed data and provide responses. These logics can evoke a simple binary response or they

may be complex models that simulate possible outcomes, weigh options, and select the most appropriate alternative. These evolving forms of interaction, coupled with new methods of digital modeling that have increased computational efficiency, require an important shift in our conceptualization of responsive technologies in association with simulation. This shift requires designers to confront two important paradigms: a compressed, autonomous modeling heuristic and a pervasive, expanding simulation space.

With regard to the first, creating models is a heuristic process that typically requires the model to be produced, executed, analyzed, and updated. Often the ground itself is assumed to be static, but phenomena such as hydrology are dynamic and varied, requiring models to predict behaviors. The process creates a feedback loop that allows the model's complexity and accuracy to evolve over successive iterations, which could occur over the course of a day or, in more complex scenarios, over weeks. As the modeler creates successive iterations, he or she learns from previous models and tunes them to represent their targets with ever-growing precision. With increased computational power and efficiency, the speed of each cycle increases, and models that simulate complex processes such as fluid dynamics or ray-traced lighting can now run faster than real time. The speed of this feedback loop can thus temporally compress the heuristic of the model, enabling the outcomes to form the basis for new relationships or predictions. The increased speed enhances the model's adaptive capacity; for example, the process of constructing topography can be evaluated as it evolves, allowing it to respond to dynamic hydrological systems.

The second conceptual shift concerns the expansion of the simulation space, particularly in its pervasiveness in control systems, which is in direct opposition to the visibility of the simulation itself. Simulation becomes invisible, a background process that mediates human interaction with machine systems and environmental phenomena. The pervasiveness of this form of simulation is directly correlated with the simulation's invisibility, performing as an extension of the sensing and response feedback cycles. This thin but powerful form of mediation creates a method of control that is as imperceptible as the interaction between physical constructions within an ecological system.

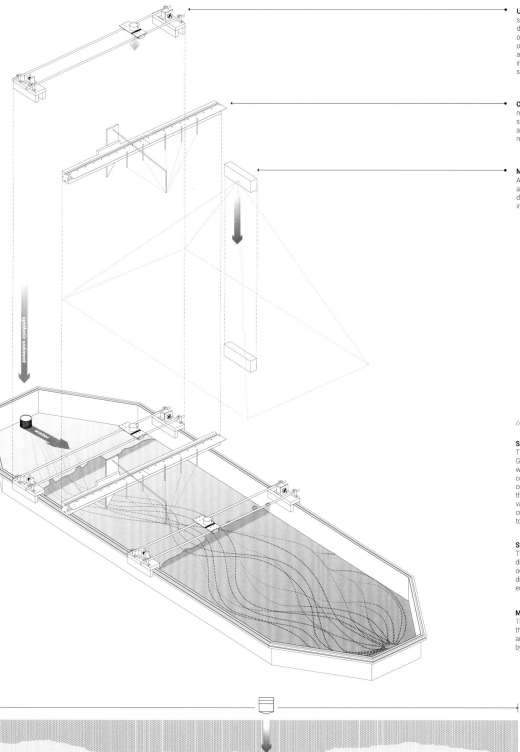

// sensing and monitoring devices

**Ultrasonic Sensors** utilize echolocation in order to extract sediment spot elevations and supply data for sectional studies. Sectional data help make informed decisions about sediment formation in order to simulate predictable scenarios. The sensors are mounted on individual custom gantries and glide back and forth on bearings across a steel rod capturing a cross section perpendicular to the inflow. The motor takes 30,000 steps to cross the table, and 30,000 steps back to compose a section.

**Capacitive Sensor** utilizes conductivity in order to detect water movement, sediment saturation, and the conductive field of the sand table. Conductivity data is utilized to track sediment saturation and draw correlations between sediment formations and water retention.

**Microsoft Kinect**
An aerial gantry carries a Microsoft Kinect to capture aerial imagery and point cloud data of the sediment bed topography. A real-time digital elevation model is generated in a custom graphical user interface as a base for real-time analysis.

// sediment bed components

**Sediment Bed**
The base for the geomorphology table is the Little River Em2 Geomodel on a tilt table. A single pump pushes varying volumes of water though the model while a vertical plastic tube on the low side controls the total volume of water in the model. The tilt table controls elevation changes from front to back and side to side of the model. The model basin is filled with three types of sediment varying in color and size. This off the shelf model is augmented with custom GUI software, hardware to run sensors, and an aerial gantry to carry sensors and cameras.

**Synthetic Sediment**
The synthetic sediment varies in color and size and is made from different densities of plastic designed to perform like naturally occuring sediments. The densities cause the particles to perform differently and the color helps to visualize resulting deposition and erosion patterns.

**Media Feeder**
The media feeder holds and distributes the synthetic sediment into the sediment bed at the inflow. The media feeder is controlled by arduino microprocessors and can be adjusted manually by dials or by scripted protocols to run various simulations.

*...extracted from the sediment bed by an ultrasonic banner sensor*

To better understand the significance of these conceptual shifts, it is helpful to review previous models of landscape simulation and control.[3] An illustrative example is the physical Mississippi Basin Model (MBM) and the subsequent computational models that were developed from it. The MBM was exceptional due to its size, the length of time invested in the modeling effort, the resulting intervention in the watershed, and the overlap with computational modeling. Model construction began in 1943 in Clinton, Mississippi as a part of the Waterways Experiment Station (WES). The effort signaled a shift in engineering that moved the discipline toward numerical modeling and laboratory models that simulated interconnected systems.[4] As Kristi Cheramie states, this was the first time that engineers, politicians, and landholders were able to comprehend their roles within the larger Mississippi River watershed through the observation of a tangible model.[5]

Although the MBM operated at the intersection of fieldwork and laboratory science, it also aligned with a post–World War II investment in infrastructure, which drastically increased the model's significance as it influenced the construction of new levees, spillways, and locks. Operationally, the MBM created a space in which to conduct sound hydrologic studies without the cost, complexity, and danger involved in manipulating the river itself. The model makers invested heavily in instrumentation and automation that allowed the feeding of historic and future scenario data into control systems. Moreover, the model was tuned through successive simulations that calibrated the surfaces, channels, and control systems to make the MBM perform in a similar manner to the historic norms of the Mississippi River. Just as importantly, the process of building the model itself was a form of inquiry, requiring the abstraction of complex systems that could be distilled to permit repeatable experiments. The model functioned operationally as a surrogate for the larger Mississippi River watershed and also provided a space where discussions between engineers and scientists, as well as presentations to politicians and stakeholders, could take place. Individuals could occupy the 1:1000 model space, stand confidently next to the simulated locations of major urban centers, and understand how engineered changes upstream would 'save' humanity from the sublime power of the river. The MBM presented a reality of a tidy Mississippi River – controllable and, most importantly, predictable. It provided a version of the river that we have subsequently manufactured in the physical world, a precursor to the watershed that our engineering prowess has produced over the past 70 years.

In the 1970s, Congress granted appropriations to study the efficacy of computer modeling as a nascent method of hydraulic simulation. These studies resulted in the MBM's replacement by the Hydraulic Engineering Centers River Analysis System (HEC-RAS), released in 1995 as a joint collaboration between the Department of Defense and the Army Corps of Engineers.[6] These computational models have been at the core of several advancements in hydraulic modeling and are still in use within the Army Corps of Engineers. This form of simulation

Previous page, left: Photograph of Mississippi Basin Model showing formed concrete panels, river channel, and mesh materials representing vegetation, Spring 2007.

Previous page, right: Drawing of fluid sediment model.

Opposite: Fluid sediment model showing various landform depositions.

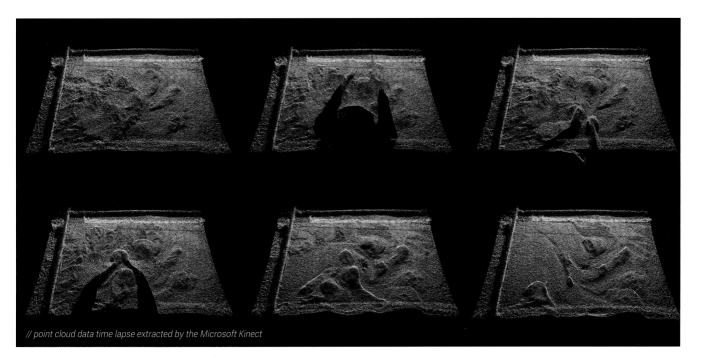

*// point cloud data time lapse extracted by the Microsoft Kinect*

is essentially the full MBM project reduced to software, with its processing occurring in real time on powerful desktop workstations.[7] This change is crucial because the feedback from simulations that previously took weeks to generate results can now be computed in microseconds and embedded into smaller and more dispersed devices. In comparison to the MBM, simulation software lacks physical tangibility but makes up for it with infinite iteration, connectivity, and portability. Computational models expand the range and speed of modeling yet, coupled with contemporary engineering paradigms and the institutions that employ such models, they remain centered on the purpose of control over hydrological systems that are inherently dynamic.[8] However, when coupled with responsive technologies, real-time (or faster than real-time) simulation provides the framework for an algorithmic heuristic. This framework in turn promotes computational learning that permits simulations and the logics that they produce to adapt as they engage ecological systems. Rather than simply seeking the most efficient macro solution, real-time simulations linked to in situ sensing devices can determine appropriate responses and enable immediate action at smaller scales.

This approach is inherent in such initiatives as the Responsive Environments and Artifacts Lab (REAL) at the Harvard Graduate School of Design that is researching methods of design that are predicated on the design of adaptive infrastructures within dynamic ecological systems. This work is taking place primarily through the use of a physical geomorphology model that simulates the flow of water and sediment across a surface. The model is not a

surrogate for any particular physical location but operates as a miniaturized landscape with a limited set of variables, i.e., water flow, sediment size, and slope. The physical model is equipped with sensors that record the surface morphology at multiple fidelities, monitor water velocities, sense moisture levels within the sediment, and capture images from multiple angles, all of which are analyzed in real time. The datasets gathered from the sensors are used to create abstractions of the sediment and water flows. Abstracting the data provides the basis for optimized representations of complex phenomena, allowing them to be visualized or interpreted by devices that modify the sediment.

The model is also equipped with a computer-controlled, two-axis platform that can be positioned within the model to manipulate the sediment flows. These manipulations alter water velocities by using interferences or resistances to curate areas of deposition and erosion. This relationship between real-time abstract models and adaptive logics produces landscapes that are the product of interactions between the robotic system and the dynamic forces of the water and sediment. The research taking place in the REAL is one example of topographic formation enabled by responsive technologies; however, there are myriad settings where the design of logics to create interactions between infrastructure and ecology can be instructive.

This approach postulates a fabrication method that engages dynamic landscapes not as a generator of landscape form but as a fluid medium. The research regards fabrication as a process of addition and subtraction that is driven by contextual cues such as surface morphology, species

movement, climate, and water speed to form dynamic terrain suitable for habitat, settlement, or production. As an adaptive infrastructure, it creates a relationship with the environment, evolving its operating logics as information from the landscape is processed. The machine evolves continually through the simulation by means of its interactions within the modeling environment, in such a way that the resultant 'form' is a product of successive tuning interactions.[9] The interactions are predicated on simple criteria such as tracking low points and high points across the surface morphology, searching for differentials in water velocity within areas of flow, and monitoring changes in sediment moisture. These criteria are then used to accomplish goals such as maintaining a distribution of low, medium, and high surface conditions with stable moisture levels to provide platforms where a diverse set of flora and fauna can take root. The system does not presume that any particular location is more important than others; instead, it acts locally to accomplish these larger goals, generating a shifting physical landscape that responds to both small and large disturbances. The process of learning is enabled through a mixture of real-time simulation and local interactions, all guided by overarching goals. The interactions are catalogued based on the general current state of the system and then redeployed when they are believed to be most effective. This means of deploying responsive technologies is further complemented by computational methods that sense and engage real-time conditions through representations that more accurately reflect the dynamics involved in the practice of landscape architecture.

As a method of fabrication, the proposed system utilizes the entropy of ecological systems to construct incrementally evolving landscapes that are the product of coordinated manipulation, curation, and choreography. In this sense, the landscape architect uses simulation to generate predictive data and reduce uncertainty about the performance and design of dynamic systems. The design and formation of the logics that guide these interactions constitute a design paradigm that embraces infrastructures governed by continual adaptation. They provide landscape architects with an important set of tools to engage territorial systems and promote the use of simulation as an intermediary. The infrastructures designed through this approach are nimble and rely on the collected information to both evaluate and engage the landscape. In much the same way as the pilot of the F-35 Joint Strike Fighter depends on technologies to augment his or her senses, the landscape architect now depends on the agency of sophisticated models that can adapt in real time. Not only will these systems be more responsive, but they will also evolve in tandem with the ecologies in which they operate.

1 Lockheed Martin, "F-35 Lightning II," https://www.f35.com/about/capabilities [accessed December 28, 2015].

2 For the future of sensing technologies in landscape architecture, see Geoff Manaugh, *Landscape Futures: Instruments, Devices and Architectural Inventions* [Barcelona: Actar D Editorial, 2012], 42.

3 E.F. Schuster, "Buffon's Needle Experiment," *American Mathematical Monthly* 81 [1974]: 26–29.

4 J.E. Foster, "History and Description of the Mississippi Basin Model," *Mississippi Basin Model Report* 1-6, US Army Corps of Engineers Waterways Experiment Station [August 1971].

5 Kristi Cheramie, "The Scale of Nature: Mississippi River Basin Model," *Places Journal* [accessed September 29, 2015].

6 US Army Corps of Engineers, "Hydrologic Engineering Center," http://www.hec.usace.army.mil/about/history.aspx [accessed December 28, 2015].

7 Richard Nance & Robert Sargent, "Perspectives on the Evolution of Simulation," *Electrical Engineering and Computer Science*, Paper 100, http://surface.syr.edu/eecs/100. [accessed December 28, 2015].

8 See James C. Scott's writings regarding how the overlap among technology, society, and the state form pervasive frameworks of control. James C. Scott, *Seeing like a State: How Certain Schemes to Improve the Human Condition Have Failed* [New Haven: Yale University Press, 1998].

9 "A key thought is that 'positive feedback,' i.e., processes and structures that mutually reinforce one another sustain dynamic and path-dependent stability regimes that shape and govern system dynamics [and thus influences localized interaction]." Henrik Ernstson, et al., "Urban Transitions: On Urban Resilience and Human-Dominated Ecosystems," *AMBIO* 39 [2010]: 531–45.

Opposite: Fluid sediment model showing sediment deposition and groundwater flow in the background and the two axis system in the foreground.

## welcome to
# "AFGHANISTAN," CA

## TO SEE HOW AMERICA'S MILITARY FIGHTERS TRAIN BEFORE THEY DEPLOY, BOOK A TOUR TODAY AND BRING YOUR CAMERA!

 ERTEBAT SHAR

# NTC BOX TOUR ITINERARY
*Offered twice monthly, free of charge\**

**09:30** Meet at Painted Rocks

**09:50** Overview of NTC operations by the Commanding General

**10:30** Guided installation tour

**11:30** Lunch at Dining Facility

**13:00** Observe Urban Situational Training Exercise at the "Box"

**14:30** Visit NTC and 11th Armored Cavalry Regiment Museum

**15:45** Return to Painted Rocks for departure

**Note**: Children under 8 are not permitted. Closed-toe shoes and protective eyewear are required; sunscreen and hats are recommended.

*\*Excluding the cost of lunch. Dining facility is cash only and no tank tops allowed. Museum gift shop accepts cash, credit, and debit cards.*

In the middle of California's high Mojave Desert, halfway between Los Angeles and Las Vegas, lies "Afghanistan." One of 11 villages within the United States Military's 1,200-acre National Training Center at Fort Irwin, the fictitious town of Ertebat Shar (formerly Medina Wasl, Iraq) plays host to elaborate simulated battle exercises as part of an intensive training program intended to prepare soldiers for Middle East combat.

In pursuit of this goal, the installation goes far beyond the physical re-creation of structures. Hundreds of role players compose the population of Ertebat Shar, including more than 350 paid civilian actors and 120 members of the United States Military who play the role of insurgents. Insurgents are held to lower grooming standards and are tasked solely with wreaking havoc, motivated by the looming consequence of being reassigned to detail elsewhere on base should they 'die' in a simulation.

Twice monthly, the public is invited to Fort Irwin for free tours, which include the opportunity to observe the Urban Situational Training Exercise at the "Box," where real amputees lose prosthetic limbs and sophisticated theatrics facilitate the detonation of suicide bombers. Visitors are encouraged to take photographs during their visit and to share them on social media.

With the US withdrawal of troops from the real Afghanistan, it is understood that the architectural character of Ertebat Shar will be redesigned and the stage-set exchanged for a new military theater.

URBAN SITUATIONAL TRAINING EXERCISE

00:02.42

00:23.49

00:27.58

00:28.06

00:51.39

01:35.47

ROBERT GERARD PIETRUSKO
# THE SURFACE OF DATA

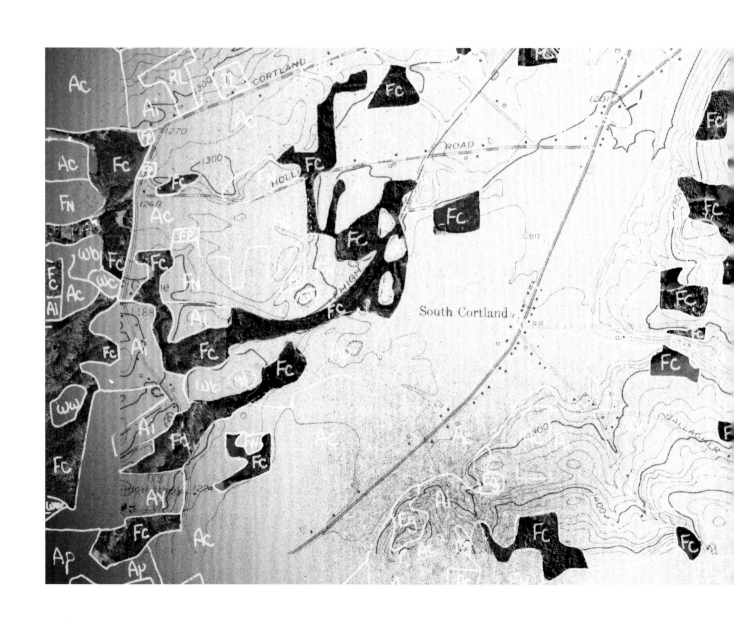

Robert Gerard Pietrusko is an Assistant Professor at Harvard University's Graduate School of Design in the Departments of Landscape Architecture and Urban Planning. His research focuses on geospatial representation, simulation, and spatial taxonomies. He is the principal of Warning Office, an experimental cartographic practice. His work has been featured at the ZKM in Karlsruhe, The Museum of Modern Art in New York, the SFMOMA in San Francisco, and most recently at the Palais De Tokyo in Paris.

+ CARTOGRAPHY, PLANNING

On June 28, 1971, the National Aeronautics and Space Administration (NASA) and the US Geological Survey (USGS) convened a three-day conference on the topic of land use information and classification. With the imminent launch of NASA's Earth Resources Technology Satellite, ERTS-1, the agencies were attempting to better understand how high-altitude imagery recorded by satellite could be used for resource management, regional planning, and geographical research in general.[1] The conference was the first project of a newly established steering committee tasked with creating a single land use classification scheme deployable at the national scale. It would provide the basic categories of land use that are now commonly used in many geospatial datasets: cropland, wetlands, high and low density development, and so on.

Dr Ernest E. Hardy of Cornell University's Center for Aerial Photographic Interpretation presented one of the conference's keynote papers. Speaking from experience gained during a recently completed study of New York State's land use, he highlighted a "major problem of concepts" in connecting satellite-based remote sensing with the creation of a land use classification scheme.

> We tend to take an existing classification system and turn to our remote sensors and ask, 'How much of this can you give us?' ... We should take the reverse approach. We should ask ourselves what information about land use can be gotten from air photos, for example, rather than designing first a comprehensive and complete land use classification and then going to the air photos to find how much information they will provide.[2]

Hardy's statement turns on its head the normally assumed order of ontology, representation, and classification. Rather than a stable set of land uses out in the world, represented with greater or less resolution, the units of land use are *defined* by the techniques of measurement (remote sensors), the materials of representation (air photos), and the process of human interpretation. A successful classification scheme parcels the world into a set of categories—and only those categories—that interpreters can repeatedly recognize in the tones and patterns of remotely sensed imagery.

With this short statement, Hardy presented the underlying epistemic conceit of geospatial data. Unlike other forms of representation, datasets assume *interpretation* and analysis as their pre-condition for being. To these ends, they are brought into registration with other datasets to produce new knowledge. In what Susan Leigh Star calls a "cascade of representations," the materiality of data conforms to standard sizes and formats, as well as conventions of measurement, recording, and documentation that make them more easily overlaid or combined. At the same time, however, fitting the data within these standards produces tension with the objects that the data represent.[3]

Additionally, the materiality of a dataset enters into the process of interpretation; these are the physical objects that are actually measured, catalogued, analyzed, debated, and ultimately translated into categories. The information contained in data is not simply a curated subset of characteristics intrinsic to the object that the data represent; it is instead constituted by the interaction between the material properties of data and the interpretation process into which it enters. Rather than treating data as a lens on the world—a lens of varying resolution and clarity—one can understand it as a surface on which the tense interaction among objects of inquiry, the banal materiality of representations, and techniques of interpretation is traced.

We can gain a better understanding of land use data through this framework by looking closely at another one of Hardy's projects that preceded the 1971 conference: the Land Use and Natural Resources Inventory of New York State (LUNR). In this project, the definition and enumeration of land use categories are of primary concern, as is the specific process of interpretation, described by Hardy as "developed on a highly pragmatic basis...rather than [to] satisfy any particular set of theoretical constructs."[4]

This paper will focus on the relationship among LUNR's representational materials, its techniques of interpretation, and the resulting categories of land use. Through the close analysis of these relationships I hope to demonstrate the following three points:

[1] The techniques of image interpretation determined the land use categories in the scheme. Rather than working with an *a priori* classification of land use activities out in the world and on the ground, the air photos themselves were the site of analysis. Only categories that could be repeatedly associated with visual patterns extracted from images were considered for the classification scheme.

[2] The process of interpretation was not a simple mapping from image to eye to category but was *shaped by the photographs and maps themselves*;[5] their methods of inventorying and their material properties defined the boundaries of work for the interpreters, as well as the hierarchy of decision making in the project regarding the appropriate list of land use categories.

[3] As a result, land use classification in LUNR was not an ontology of the ground, as we might conventionally assume, but rather an epistemology of the lab.[6]

Between 1966 and 1971, New York State's Office of Planning Coordination (OPC) commissioned Cornell University's Center for Aerial Photographic Interpretation to conduct an inventory that would "assess and portray the present extent, character,

and uses of the land and water resources" for the entire state.[7] A legible dataset representing the amount of land devoted to different land uses and their distribution among the counties was desired in order to make better management decisions at both state and county levels. Given the ambitious spatial extent of the inventory, traditional methods of enumeration, such as on-the-ground field surveys, were not feasible; instead, the Cornell team proposed analysis of aerial photography under Hardy's direction.

LUNR was a process of many material translations. The ground was successively abstracted into representational forms that could circulate among multiple state agencies and be employed in arbitrary, user-defined analyses.[8] A team of 50 photo interpreters visually classified 15,000 black-and-white aerial images; the continuous tones and patterns of the images were delineated into discrete land use categories drafted onto Mylar maps. These maps were overlaid with a one-kilometer grid through which the land use areas were hand-aggregated onto spreadsheets and ultimately entered into a computer database from which a virtually limitless number of custom maps could be derived. The land use areas for the entire state could be represented in a single table, as could arbitrary comparisons between any number of counties.[9]

At the heart of the project was the definition of LUNR's land use categories – the initial translation from continuous visual patterns in aerial images to discrete and countable entities. The design of these categories and of the workflow for their interpretation constituted a major component of the project's development and was prominently documented over its duration.[10] Therefore, to understand how the relationship between the physical materials of representation and human interpretation asserted its influence on the categories, a close and detailed reading of the process is required.

## Classifying

LUNR's land use categorization began with a list provided by OPC in 1966. It included land, water, minerals, and five other categories of generally defined natural resources. Within five years, this number would grow to 81.[11] In the design of the land use classification, previous schemes were considered, notably the Standard Land Use Coding Manual (SLUC) developed by the federal government's Urban Renewal Administration in 1965. Containing over 700 categories of human land use, the SLUC was comprehensive by any measure and was specifically designed for inventories like LUNR.[12] Despite this, Hardy and his team deemed it unusable for a process based on aerial photo interpretation, citing both the density of categories and the length of the codes themselves, i.e., the number of alphanumeric characters needed to signify a land use.[13] The SLUC divided land use in a manner not easily discerned in the tone and pattern of an air photo, and the lengthy codes were difficult to map by hand; the number of characters simply would not fit within the regions that they described. The rejection of SLUC demonstrates that, at an early stage, the material properties of images, maps, hands, and pencils were already shaping decisions regarding the appropriate categories to use in the project. LUNR's land use categories were instead designed within the photo interpretation lab.

In February 1967, the team received a collection of air photos covering New York's Cortland County. Each image was photographed in black and white at a scale of 1:24,000 and developed in a 9x9-inch format.[14] On a table in the center of the lab, the images were layered into a mosaic – an overlapping matrix of individual images covering a larger land area. The team gathered around the table and began identifying various visual patterns. Each pattern was assigned a land use name, and a running list of those under consideration was maintained and modified on the lab blackboard. Thus, the classification of land use *began* with the process of interpreting the images, rather than from the ground itself. Over the course of two months, the team all "gradually began to agree" on what these land use categories should be. Indeed, "many of those decisions were made as [they] stood around the map mosaic of the pilot area, using it as a continual reference and focus for discussion."[15] Rather than concerning themselves with a mimetic correspondence to the land uses generally perceived as existing by on-the-ground observers, the team judged its progress with a different set of criteria. Within the continuous visual sensation of the images, what combination of tone and texture constituted a pattern? Could the pattern be repeatedly identified across a team of interpreters? Where should discrete boundaries between the patterns be drawn? Once the surface of the image has been fully delineated, to what categories should the patterns be assigned? An interpretive consensus determined how the space of land use would be defined. The images gradually became data.

Despite the team's general agreement on the land use categories in its first two months of photo analysis, the scheme was revised 12 times during the project.[16] The feasibility of each land use category on the blackboard was continually judged against the ongoing interpretation workflow developed alongside them: "Discussions of the techniques for the inventory had paralleled, influenced, and been influenced by the development of the classification. The techniques for the most part evolved in that same lab room."[17] While the tones and patterns of the imagery determined the initial space of possible land use categories, these categories were further shaped by the specificity of a rigorously organized interpretation process. As this process evolved, so did the official list of land uses.

To be clear, the work described here did not simply involve accurately classifying images into pre-established categories. Instead, the process of classifying images, when distributed across a team, revealed that some categories produced uncertainty and error more frequently than others. This lack of consensus, specifically related to the materials and organization of the interpretation process, caused the modification of land use categories.

## Interpreting

Photo interpretation in LUNR might at first appear to be a straightforward translation from the continuous tones and patterns in an air photo to the discrete boundaries of a land use map. However, the act of interpretation itself was strictly defined in relation to the material properties of the images and maps as well as the interaction among several institutional time scales in the project. These factors structured the work of the interpreters and, through their performance, redefined the set of land use categories.

Underlying the project's workflow was a collection of USGS topographic base maps that parcel the country into an evenly spaced, 7.5-minute degree grid of latitude and longitude. Each of the grid cells–or quadrangles–is given a unique location code and associated with a 24x36-inch standalone topographic map.[18] Both the unique location code and the physical map were important determinants in the interpretation workflow [opposite].

First, the map location codes provided an organizational structure through which all the media in the project were catalogued. For instance, aerial photos were initially received by the lab in linear 'flight strips.' Following the original path of the plane that recorded the imagery, the order of the photos corresponded to contiguous areas on the ground. However, once they reached the lab, the photographs were "sorted and filed by USGS topographic maps...according to the location of their principal [central] points."[19] Images contained within a quadrangle were removed from the original flight strip and stored together as a group, labeled by the quadrangle's unique code.[20] As a result, the original spatial adjacencies and contiguous ground area among the images were disrupted, as were any land use patterns depicted across multiple image boundaries.[21] As I will explain shortly, this disruption resulted in error-checking procedures that were important for the continual modification of land use categories.

Second, the 24x36-inch surface of a topographic map defined the work boundary for an individual interpreter. Working on the imagery within a single quadrangle at a time, the interpreter retained authority over it through its numerous translations, from imagery to categories to computer code. Beginning with a single quadrangle, the interpreter arranged multiple air photos into alignment with its borders and features. Then, drawing directly on the photographs with a wax pencil, he or she delineated bounded image patterns and assigned them land use codes.[22] Within the boundaries of the topographic map, interpreters had full authority to determine the appropriate land use categories.[23]

However, the boundaries *between* adjacent maps produced a different organizational logic and directly connected the individual interpreters' work to the hierarchy of decision making and the modification of the land use categories. As an

1 James Anderson, *Proceedings of the Conference on Land Use Information and Classification* [Washington, DC: United States Geological Survey, 1971].

2 Ibid., 50.

3 Susan Leigh Star, "The Politics of Formal Representations: Wizards, Gurus, and Organizational Complexity," in Star [ed] *Ecologies of Knowledge: Work and Politics in Science and Technology* [Albany: State University of New York Press, 1985], 88–118.

4 Ernest Hardy, et al., *New York State Land Use and Natural Resources Inventory: Final Report Volume 2* [Ithaca, NY: Cornell University Center for Aerial Photographic Interpretation, 1971], 4.

5 James Gibson, *The Ecological Approach to Visual Perception* [London: Lawrence Erlbaum, 1986].

6 Ian Hacking, *Representing and Intervening: Introductory Topics in the Philosophy of Natural Science* [Cambridge: Cambridge University Press, 1983].

7 Donald Belcher, et al., *New York State Land Use and Natural Resources Inventory: Final Report Volume 1* [Ithaca, NY: Cornell University Center for Aerial Photographic Interpretation, 1971], 6.

8 Star, "The Politics of Formal Representations."

9 Hardy, et al. *New York State Land Use*, 17.

10 Raymond Kreig, "Aerial Photographic Interpretation for Land Use Classification in the New York State Land Use and Natural Resources Inventory," *Photogrammetria* 26, no. 2 [1970]; Ronald Shelton & Ernest Hardy, "Design Concepts for Land Use and Natural Resource Inventories and Information Systems," *International Symposium on Remote Sensing of Environment* [1974]; Hardy, et al., *New York State Land Use.*

11 Hardy, ibid., 24–40.

12 United States Urban Renewal Administration, *Standard Land Use Coding Manual: A Standard System for Identifying and Coding Land Use Activities* [Washington, DC: U.S. Govt. Printing Office, 1965].

13 Hardy, et al., *New York State Land Use*, 12.

14 Ibid., 14.

15 Ibid., 69.

16 Ibid.

17 Ibid.

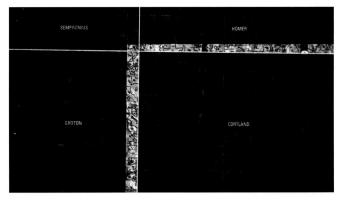

interpreter layered a mosaic of 9x9-inch aerial photos within a 24x36-inch topographic map, the images did not fit neatly within the map's boundary; the pattern of the images drifted across the borders of multiple maps, and therefore into the geographic areas assigned to multiple interpreters. The borders themselves were sites of competing work since, in addition to a map's interior, interpreters were expected to classify land uses along a one-inch margin beyond its north and west edges.[24] Patterns on a single image straddled adjacent maps and were therefore classified by separate interpreters at different times, producing discrepancies in both the perceived categories and the location of their boundaries.

LUNR's organizational chart was structured in response to the material misalignment between the jurisdiction of the interpreters–defined by the quadrangle's boundaries–and the images on which they worked. A new role, that of the 'tie-in specialist,' was created with the sole task of managing and resolving the differences between adjacent maps and competing interpreters. When discrepancies were found in the map margins, the tie-in specialist had full authority to decide the appropriate categories and their extents.[25] This had two effects: interpreters deemed to be in error would be retrained on the proper classification, or, if a category was found to be repeatedly problematic and interpreters could not establish consensus in its application, it was changed and the classification scheme was updated (above).

## Perceiving

The categories and the interpretation process were entangled in other profound ways, notably, in the measure of classification speed and the inscribing of visual uncertainty on the landscape. This was due to the highly specific definition given to 'interpretation' within the project:

> [LUNR] does not require true 'photo interpretation' which requires highly-trained deductive and inductive evaluation of the air photo patterns. Instead, this project only requires 'photo reading' which involves simple recognition making the classification time very small (a matter of seconds).[26]

The difference between interpretation and recognition was established as being about 10 to 15 seconds per category.[27] If the interpreter could classify a land use within 15 seconds it was in the realm of recognition. Categories that required more time were considered interpretation. Even though more nuanced information could possibly be gathered from a process of detailed inspection, the classification scheme was designed to optimize speed by defining classes that the interpreters could more easily distinguish.[28]

The interpreter still required observational powers to decide among a variety of visual sensations and patterns, but the discrete boundaries between them, along with their land use labels, were determined elsewhere in the project hierarchy.

Furthermore, the division between photo reading and photo interpretation–between perception and judgment–was reflected in the land use categories themselves. So-called 'wastebasket classes' were included at each level of the schema to collect patterns requiring longer classification times.[29] Despite their common names, such as "[Fc] Brushland," wastebasket classes curtailed an interpreter's mental transition from perception to judgment, and they translated the boundary of a perceptual process into a boundary of land use, registered back onto the landscape (p. 78-9).

## Conclusion

LUNR's categories and interpretation process were important precursors to the national and global land use datasets that emerged alongside the field of satellite-based sensing. Along with geographer James Anderson, Ernest Hardy ultimately co-authored the official land use classification scheme debated at the USGS/NASA conference. *A Land Use Classification System for Use with Remote Sensor Data* was published by the USGS in 1972, and again in a revised form in 1976.[30] The highly specific title–claiming data as the object of classification–is not incidental; many of Hardy's findings from LUNR were deeply embedded in the scheme. This system has provided the criteria and categories for every comprehensive US land cover dataset released since its circulation and, therefore, has formed the basis for numerous simulations of land use dynamics, urban growth, and resource depletion.[31]

LUNR is important not only because of this lineage but also because it highlights a shift in focus, from ground to lab, that occurred with new methods of sensing and the need to interpret contemporary land use as data. The categories used to create discrete classes from continuous imagery were optimized for repeatable, standardized interpretability within the lab, rather than emerging from a concern for accurate representations of the ground. Furthermore, this process of interpretation was influenced by specific organizational workflows in relation to the representational materials themselves. Exploring these organizational and material conditions of data opens them to continued experimentation and review while, at the same time, discounting the claims of those who would treat these datasets as raw data and outside the realm of debate.

18 Patrick H. McHaffie, "Towards the Automated Map Factory: Early Automation at the U.S. Geological Survey," *Cartography and Geographic Information Science* 29, no. 3 (2002): 193–206.

19 Hardy, et al., *New York State Land Use*, 93.

20 Ronald Shelton, *Technical Manual* (Ithaca, NY: Cornell University Center for Aerial Photographic Interpretation, 1967), II–1.

21 This reordering was necessary to manage the materiality of thousands of nearly identical-looking photographs and relate them to specific map locations.

22 Hardy, et al., *New York State Land Use*, 99.

23 Ibid., 105.

24 Ibid.

25 Ibid.

26 Kreig, "Aerial Photographic Interpretation," 103.

27 Roger Swanson, *The Land Use and Natural Resources Inventory of New York State* (Albany: New York State Office of Planning Coordination, 1969).

28 Ibid., 104.

29 Kreig, "Aerial Photographic Interpretation," 107.

30 James Anderson, et al., *A Land Use and Land Cover Classification System for Use with Remote Sensor Data* (Washington, DC: US Geological Survey, 1976).

31 Mario Gomarasca, *Basics of Geomatics* (Dordrecht: Springer Netherlands, 2008), 561–98; James Vogelmann, et al., "Completion of the 1990s National Land Cover Data Set for the Conterminous United States From Landsat Thematic Mapper Data and Ancillary Data Sources," *Photogrammetric Engineering and Remote Sensing* 67, no. 6 (2001): 650–62.

# SENSING THE EARTH

Curiosity about the Earth has led humans to develop many types of remote sensing instruments to help us uncover the complexities of the environment that lies beyond our immediate perception. The early days of hydrological surveying used handheld lead lines to measure water depth. Later, single-beam and multi-beam echo sounders were developed to measure the depth between the ocean floor and surface. Early aerial photography, for both scientific and military purposes, used hot-air balloons, kites, and pigeons. Our perspective on the Earth has continued to reach greater and greater heights with the progression from airplanes to rockets to satellites. The extension of humans' sensory limits through the use of instruments continues to open new horizons of understanding and has led to an increased ability to visualize the complex physical processes that constitute our environment. By making the 'invisible' visible, remote sensing impacts what we see and, therefore, what we know about the world around us.

**1858**
HOT-AIR BALLOON WITH CAMERA
FIRST KNOWN AERIAL PHOTOGRAPH

**1882**
KITE WITH CAMERA

1800    1810    1820    1830    1840    1850    1860    1870    1880

**1807**
US OFFICE OF COAST SURVEY ESTABLISHED

**1834**
LEAD LINE

INSTRUMENTS: HOT-AIR BALLOON WITH CAMERA

INSTRUMENTS: KITE WITH CAMERA

INSTRUMENTS: PIGEON WITH CAMERA

INSTRUMENTS: AIRPLANE WITH CAMERA

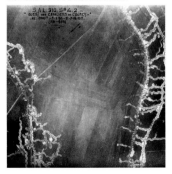

Sources: "History of Aerial Photography" www.professionalaerialphotographers.com/content.aspx?page_id=22&club_id=808138&module_id=158950; "NASA Remote Sensing Accomplishments" http://earthobservatory.nasa.gov/Features/RemoteSensing/remote_09.php; "History of Hydrographic Surveying" http://www.nauticalcharts.noaa.gov/hsd/hydro_history.html.

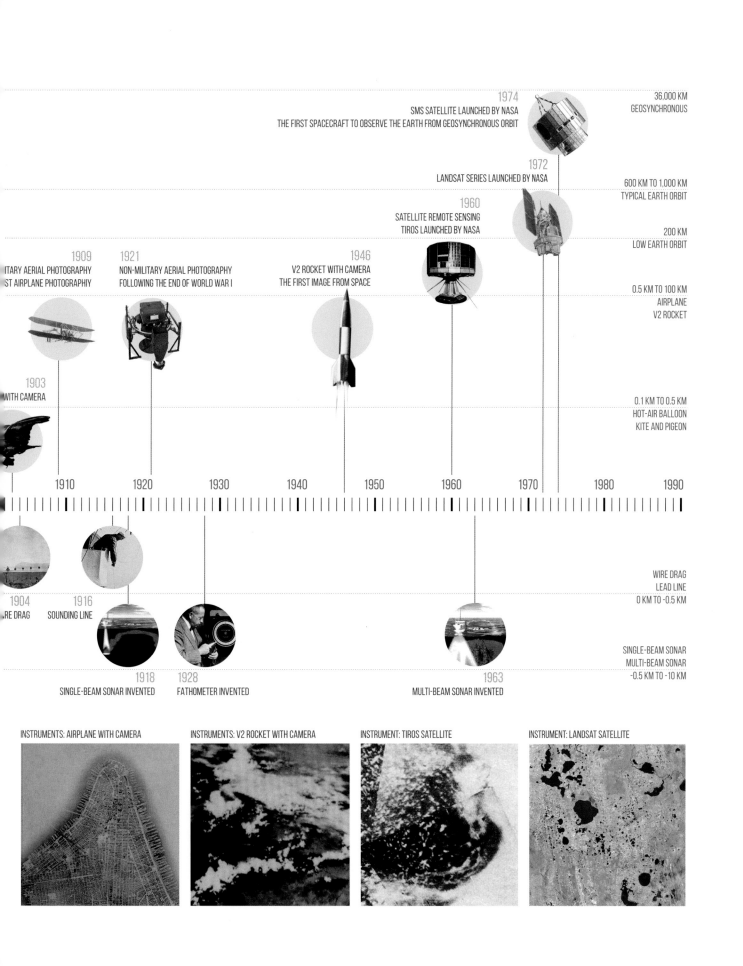

1974
SMS SATELLITE LAUNCHED BY NASA
THE FIRST SPACECRAFT TO OBSERVE THE EARTH FROM GEOSYNCHRONOUS ORBIT

36,000 KM
GEOSYNCHRONOUS

1972
LANDSAT SERIES LAUNCHED BY NASA

600 KM TO 1,000 KM
TYPICAL EARTH ORBIT

1960
SATELLITE REMOTE SENSING
TIROS LAUNCHED BY NASA

200 KM
LOW EARTH ORBIT

1909
ITARY AERIAL PHOTOGRAPHY
ST AIRPLANE PHOTOGRAPHIY

1921
NON-MILITARY AERIAL PHOTOGRAPHY
FOLLOWING THE END OF WORLD WAR I

1946
V2 ROCKET WITH CAMERA
THE FIRST IMAGE FROM SPACE

0.5 KM TO 100 KM
AIRPLANE
V2 ROCKET

1903
WITH CAMERA

0.1 KM TO 0.5 KM
HOT-AIR BALLOON
KITE AND PIGEON

1910     1920     1930     1940     1950     1960     1970     1980     1990

WIRE DRAG
LEAD LINE
0 KM TO -0.5 KM

1904
RE DRAG

1916
SOUNDING LINE

SINGLE-BEAM SONAR
MULTI-BEAM SONAR
-0.5 KM TO -10 KM

1918
SINGLE-BEAM SONAR INVENTED

1928
FATHOMETER INVENTED

1963
MULTI-BEAM SONAR INVENTED

INSTRUMENTS: AIRPLANE WITH CAMERA

INSTRUMENTS: V2 ROCKET WITH CAMERA

INSTRUMENT: TIROS SATELLITE

INSTRUMENT: LANDSAT SATELLITE

# IN CONVERSATION WITH
# KOERT VAN MENSVOORT

*Papilio Nike-Ulysses (USA)*

**Dr Koert van Mensvoort** is an artist and philosopher best known for his work on the philosophical concept of Next Nature, which posits that our technological environment has become so complex, omnipresent, and autonomous that it is best perceived as a nature of its own. It is his aim to better understand our co-evolutionary relationship with technology and help set out a track toward a future that is rewarding for both humankind and the planet at large. LA+ spoke with Koert about how various forms of simulation are reshaping the relationship between nature and technology, and about the role of old nature in Next Nature.

+ How do you define simulation, or dissimulation, within the context of your work?

I try to stick to the normal, everyday definition: imitation of some real world process that is already there. It becomes a bit more complicated, of course, because then you have a distinction between the 'real' world and the simulation. But that is thinking of reality and simulation in terms of how Plato thought it. Aristotle had another view, which was not about the opposition between simulation and reality. He said that through mimesis we learn to meet reality. I very much subscribe to that position.

+ So should we consider simulations as mediators or representations, or have they become a reality or truth unto themselves?

In my view, simulations define part of our reality. How we see reality, or the concept of reality, is much more related to the concept of authority than we typically realize. This is quite important because, for instance, if you look at a phenomenon like gravity, that has an enormous reality. I can jump as much as I like but I will always be pulled back through gravity. That's very real. But it also has great authority.

If we see parallels with the virtual world as we define it—digital worlds and virtual realties—they often start as some extra layer on our lives, but at certain moments, they gain an authority that becomes so strong that we cannot move away from it anymore. They become a reality. As they gain the authority, they also enforce their reality.

+ Rather than an interpretation of nature as something autonomous and unaltered, your work addresses a state in which real and artificial are no longer separate. What's the role of the old nature in Next Nature?

The role of old nature is still very important because it is our history. It's where we come from and I think we can still learn a lot from old nature in order to cope better with the Next Nature. We should stop seeing nature as a static entity - as a perfect world that used to exist, and that used to be balanced and harmonic before mankind arrived and started spoiling everything. Although that idea is quite strong, it's a fiction. Nature has never been static; it was always a dynamic force, a dynamic reality, and it changes along with us. Time after time we struggle with old nature and in that conversation with old nature, we transform it, and we turn it into Next Nature. And what is Next Nature today might be the old nature in some future. What is artificial today might be considered natural tomorrow.

+ So, do you think the notion of preservation is the wrong frame of mind or does it have a role?

I think preservation is not the wrong notion but it should not be clinging onto a static past. We should more see it as cultural heritage.

That's a slightly different agenda than simply saying we should stick to what we thought was the world before mankind arrived. I don't want to go back to nature, I want to go forward to nature, and that means you can take things from the past but they will always transform in the future.

To give a concrete example, Stewart Brand is working on not just preserving species, but also regenerating extinct species. This makes very visible that preservation is static – if you bring back extinct species then you are creating a completely new situation even though you're bringing something back. This is a different approach to biodiversity and preservation. I would say this is an innovative nostalgic approach that is more interesting than simply saying we should freeze everything and stick to what it was.

+ A recent op-ed in the LA Times by Joshua Galperin remarked on his students' diminished interest in calling themselves "environmentalists." With this, he worries that the successes of the original environmental movement in the United States (e.g. Clean Water Act) will be impossible to maintain or repeat. While Next Nature is a vital conceptual reframing, is it actionable? Can it shape environmental policies?

Yes. The Next Nature philosophy should be actionable because any philosophy, at a certain point, has to be actionable, and I feel responsible for that to a certain extent. The actions we should take around Next Nature relate to the observation that we not only have a biosphere, we also have a technosphere, which is the sum of all human technologies that have evolved upon the biosphere. Just as the biosphere evolved upon the geosphere and interacts with the geosphere, the technosphere evolves upon the biosphere and interacts with it. It's our responsibility to find a balance in these spheres because we are the catalyst in the middle and it is there that we can take action.

+ Do you have an example of something you are working on now?

I'm presently working on an eco-currency – a currency for environmental value. It started with the simple observation that all money is virtual; if you look into the history of humankind then you see that money has become increasingly intangible. It's an example of a virtual reality that is very tangible in all our lives. What if we could make a currency that is linked to things that are actually most valuable in life? It would not be gold but rather ecological entities like clean water and trees that eat carbon dioxide. Imagine a Brazilian farmer in the rainforest: their only choice is to cut down trees, plant soy, and make money or let the trees be and earn nothing.

We have to develop a currency that values these trees, and then we can pay this Brazilian farmer in eco-coins to maintain the trees and maybe even plant trees. How do you pay for that? You put a micro-tax on financial transactions because in the current financial system, in the technosphere, computers are doing over 80 percent of the trading. If we put a tax on that of 0.0001 percent it will not be noticed but the computerized algorithms that are doing thousands of financial transactions per second will be taxed. We can get a lot of money from that to front an eco-coin that we then distribute among the people who are working to benefit our environment. In order to distribute the eco-coins fairly we will need a Wikipedia-like system in which people attribute the ecological value of different activities. Of course people will try to corrupt the system, just like with Wikipedia, but they have proven such a wisdom of the crowd 'truth' system can be realized in a robust way.

+ That's interesting because it's ecosystems that we've been trying to quantify in terms of ecosystem services, but that's probably still quite abstract and intangible to most people.

Absolutely. All of the things happening around ecosystem services or nature services, and $CO_2$ trading, are organized by bureaucrats and technocrats, who assume their systems are too difficult and abstract to explain to a general audience. Partly this is true, because the general audience still has this rather naïve and romanticized notion of nature as the static untouched Paradise. I believe that a more dynamic perspective on nature, in which people understand the biosphere evolved on the geosphere some billion years ago, and with the arrival of people a technosphere evolved on the biosphere. Evolution goes on. Once this perspective gains popularity, it becomes easier to explain things like, "Let's make an eco-coin," and actually make some progress.

+ In your article "A Society of Simulations" you argue that media technologies are increasingly attaining levels of authority with that of the 'real.' What are your thoughts on the epistemology of computer simulation, especially in regard to its role studying complex phenomena?

The first that springs to mind when I hear that question is the hole in the ozone layer. At first, scientists thought that their measurements on the ozone layer were wrong. They thought, "Our devices must be broken. The models must be wrong because this cannot be happening." They really thought something was not working with their measurement process and spent a lot of time repairing their tools. Others, at first, just ignored it and thought that it was an artifact of the model or instruments. They did the measurements again and only then did they realize that there was indeed a hole in the ozone layer.

This is an example of the tension between the map and the territory, or you could also say the database and physical world. Maybe it's more a case today but the physical world cannot always support the database, like the territory cannot always support the map. This again goes back to this notion of reality and authority. We put a lot of authority in our models but sometimes it turns out that their authority is limited and a stronger reality marches in. This is something that we have to be very aware of and thus teach students database or code literacy.

+ In *Objectivity*, Lorraine Daston and Peter Galison note that with the rise of nanosciences image-as-recording has evolved into image-as-process; we have moved from image as a representation of something 'out there' to image that has no fidelity to 'what is,' thus marking the moment when nature merges with artifact. How might this relate to how you define various 'media schemas,' some of which are so embedded that they go without notice?

I think this is quite exciting that people are thinking of how the nanosciences and nanotechnologies might have this effect to the point that our environment becomes the interface and we don't have a distinction anymore between something that's real, like the grass around me, which I perceive in a different way than the computer screen in front of me, which is supposedly an image, and thus has a different quality, and a different being, than this physical thing behind me.

But if they blend, if the grass also becomes the interface and image, then indeed, that would be the ultimate crossover between artifice and nature. These technologies might force us to move away from distinctions of what is fake versus real, artificial versus natural and the media schemas have to be updated quickly enough in order for us to cope with such changes. Babies don't require updated media schemas because they're born in a world in which things that are designed are their reality and that's it. It's fascinating, for instance, when you see babies sitting on magazines trying to pinch its pages in the same manner they do on an iPad because in their media schema pinching is a means of control. You see that every generation is born in a world that functions in a certain way, which is not new because previous generations had to get used to photographs, moving images, and the like. I think that it's very important to have respect and understand about the different ways in which people are coping with media.

+ My favorite example in your book *Next Nature*, in this respect, is the girl who on her first trip to the forest remarks to her father "Daddy! The forest smells like shampoo!"

Yes. This is a very important example because your first response is to judge the child and say, "Oh, what a sad thing. She's foiled by a society of media and consumption." But I want to stress that we have to understand the child's perspective, and try to learn from that situation, and then we can make a judgment. But first, let's start with understanding and respecting it because things are changing. There are differences in the generations and with that our collective ideas about nature are changing with it.

+ In *Next Nature* you write that much of what we think is nature is a simulation – that our landscapes are creations based on an idealized image of nature. Landscape architecture frequently derives its expression from such interpretations of nature. Might you speculate on how Next Nature imagery might be a productive referent for future landscape aesthetics?

I'm not a landscape architect, so the easy thing for me to say is that it's for the landscape architects to solve. However, I do have some fantasies.

I'm from the Netherlands, and we invented landscape paintings in the 17th century. At a certain moment, these artists taught us to appreciate landscape to the level in which we now design whole landscapes according to landscape paintings. So, in Oostvaardersplassen Nature Reserve we took land from the ocean to develop a nature resort, which basically looked like the landscape paintings as we knew them. This is like Disneyland for grownups. The task that should be given to a city planner or a landscape architect is not to simulate the visual surface but the principle.

What does it feel like to be in a forest in the middle of an urban landscape? How can you work with sounds, not mimicking birds but making special soundscapes that show you where the Wi-Fi networks are, for example? The sounds are artificial but might feel natural to our senses.

A quite different scenario is the hyper-natural scenario, like the movie *Avatar*, where you live in the forest in which everything glows, everything is interactive. Imagine replacing street lights with trees that glow in the dark. It's not something that ever existed in the world, but it might be a nice place to live.

+ What's next for Next Nature?

The next step is to make a 21st-century movement called the Next Nature Network. We want to go forward to nature. Our goals are quite simple: we want to share a richer understanding of nature.

The common view of nature is still quite naïve. We want to connect the biosphere and the technosphere because the technosphere is Next Nature. While the biosphere—the old nature that is threatened—needs to be rescued, at the same time, this technosphere is quite vibrant but, to a certain extent, is threatening not only to the biosphere but also to humanity. Through our technology, we rushed into a situation where we have become so influential on our world. We need to domesticate that. We need to save the panda, but also, humanity. That is something I strive for because humanity is the most beautiful thing that I know of.

# CLAUDIA PASQUERO + MARCO POLETTO

# CYBER-GARDENING THE CITY

Claudia Pasquero is director of the Urban Morphogenesis Lab at the Bartlett in London and Senior Staff at IAAC in Barcelona. She is currently an Adapt-r research fellow investigating the cultural relevance of bio-computation at the Tallinn School of Architecture in Estonia. Together with Marco Poletto, she co-founded ecoLogicStudio in London. The studio has an international reputation for its innovative work, which integrates systemic thinking, computational design, bio-hacking and digital prototyping. Pasquero has lectured internationally and is widely published.

Marco Poletto is an architect, author, and educator. He is currently an Adapt-r research fellow in bio-digital design at the Aarhus School of Architecture in Denmark and is Distinguished Visiting Critic at Carnegie Mellon University. Poletto has published widely, his most recent book being *Systemic Architecture: Operating Manual for the Self-Organizing City* [co-authored with Claudia Pasquero].

**+** ARCHITECTURE, TECHNOLOGY, URBAN STUDIES

Opposite: Urban Algae Folly for EXPO Milano 2015.

Following page: Metropolitan Proto-Garden vegetation density map. A simulated plan of Virtual Plots and Operational Fields were developed in Grasshopper for Rhino using data extrapolated from various sources including Google Earth, Panoramio pictures and Open data Milano [2009].

Contemporary environmentalism often seems unable to escape its ideological pitfalls and recognize the inextricable complexity of our techno-human condition, along with the implications of that complexity for the natural environment. Cities, humans' biggest and most extraordinary invention, remain, from this perspective, antagonistic toward nature, and their re-greening is consistently portrayed as obligatory to rebalance their impact on the biosphere. This paper will use the case study of Milan, and ecoLogicStudio's recent work there, to make a twofold statement. First, we demonstrate the historical and scientific fallacies of the aforementioned ideological approach to urban design and architecture, and the misunderstandings to which these lead. Second, we propose a radical bio-digital understanding of urbanization using the notion of cyber-gardening the city, and we describe its actualization in a novel bio-digital architectural prototype, namely the Urban Algae Folly at the Expo Milano 2015 site.

### The eco-ideology

Few people realize that Milan is Italy's second largest agricultural municipality.[1] Many urban farms still dot its peri-urban territory, creating a web that extends all around the city's southern edge to the Expo site, an area now named the Parco Sud. This peculiar characteristic has favored a strand of rhetoric that likes to portray the agricultural area of Milan as the new ecological frontier of the city, with features varying from the picturesque [in the most peripheral farms, seen as agro-tourist or agro-cultural retreats immersed in nature and enjoying a secular balance with it] to the agro-chic [in the more urban locations, typically transformed into fashionable organic eateries].

While progressive in appearance, both tendencies are deeply conservative in character and respond to the global rhetoric of contemporary environmentalism, which leaves them unable to escape the ideological conception of nature as a fundamentally balanced and benign system currently perturbed and unsettled by urban proliferation. This narrative ignores the fact that nature is not a fundamentally balanced system. Our current techno-human condition, largely the product of industrialization and technological development, has been fueled by the discovery of an enormous reservoir of energy. This energy has been stored in the form of crude oil and other fossil fuels, themselves the product of one of the largest catastrophes in the history of the earth, which occurred eons before humans appeared. The biomass resulting from mass extinctions and the widespread destruction and death of organisms was trapped under many strata of rock for millions of years until our civilization figured out a way to access and use it.

The fallacy of the eco-ideological viewpoint also has implications for the interpretation of history. Industrialization is often portrayed as the breaking point, the moment when society became disconnected from nature and when nature's human-made perturbation began. The logical consequence of this view, as exemplified by the case of Milan, is an idealization of the Arcadian character of agriculturalism, where the pastoral scene of the urban farm is elevated to a symbol of a possible return to life in balance with nature, in contrast to the disconnected urban life – a product of industrialization.

In this respect, Milan's case is pertinent for two reasons. First, in the panorama of the Italian Renaissance, Milan reached its peak under the Sforza family who, under pressure to expand their territory, enacted an agricultural revolution. High demand to feed a growing population fueled a technological acceleration that involved the likes of Leonardo Da Vinci (who built a large network of canals, the current Navigli), farmhouses (today's Parco Sud), and productive terrains (still known as *marcite* or meadows). This preindustrial yet profoundly technological landscape dramatically increased the productivity of the land, which became in this metabolic sense urban or, as we would say today, part of the urban ecological footprint of Milan. The challenge to make Milan virtually self-sufficient transformed its urban landscape into a productive machine, a large apparatus mediating between the increasing metabolism of the city and the local landscape's natural ability to support such demands. If this was an Arcadia, it was surely a techno-human one.

This observation highlights the second point derived from Milan's case, which is the scientific fallacy of conservationism and environmentalism when applied to architecture (as in the case of urban farms now restored as relics of a rural past), landscape (as in the case of the *marcite*, now green patches of natural landscape to be protected from urbanization at any cost), its products (organic produce, today's overpriced gourmet raw material for the few), food (slow food, a trademark of the rhetoric of localism) and cooking (the rural chic gets a Michelin star). This interpretation not only fails to recognize the ambitions of those who built the original infrastructures, landscapes, and architectures of Milan's rural past, but also fails to actualize their relevance as part of the contemporary urban metabolism of the city and its metropolitan area. As a consequence, no effort is made to quantitatively assess and evaluate the landscape's capacity to feed contemporary Milan or to speculate as to what kind of transformation would be required to achieve that goal. None of the recent interventions represented in the Parco Sud, Darsena (the city's harbor), Navigli, or Expo Milano 2015 have demonstrated a clear attempt to engage the problem of the urban footprint from a radically technological point of view.[2] It should now be clear to all that the eco-ideological approach does nothing to advance our society's ability to evolve a more sophisticated paradigm of eco-systemic urbanization, as demonstrated by the incapacity of Expo Milano 2015 to address the core topic articulated in its brand title, "Feeding the planet: energy for life."

## Urbansphere as augmented biosphere

If we instead consider the actuality of our techno-human condition, we will realize that our society cannot exist outside the technological paradigm, which is best expressed in the complexity and richness of contemporary cities. Our best hope to engage this complexity is to move even farther away from nature and develop a completely abstract, mathematical description of urbanity – that is, to shift the urban design discourse into the territory of pure simulation. In this regard, we have formulated the term 'Urbansphere' to define the global network of information, matter, and energy that underpins our new, abstract model of urbanity. We claim that the Urbansphere is our real contemporary biosphere, not its antithesis. Simulated abstraction represents our fundamental living habitat, the one that we must develop for good purposes to support a prosperous future.

Departing from the fiction of environmentalism, we propose the convergence of information and biological technologies as our best chance to achieve such a goal, to evolve the Urbansphere into an augmented biosphere to such an extent that nature and its simulated artificial representation are simply part of a single co-evolutionary whole. This implies the exploitation of any opportunity that may arise in the indexing of the urban landscape and in the reinterpretation of known architectural or landscape typologies.

The reframing of types also goes hand in hand with the introduction of two key notions: the prototype, intended as a conceptual space of design simulation that exists above or beyond its categorization as a type; and the operational field, an abstract and mathematical description

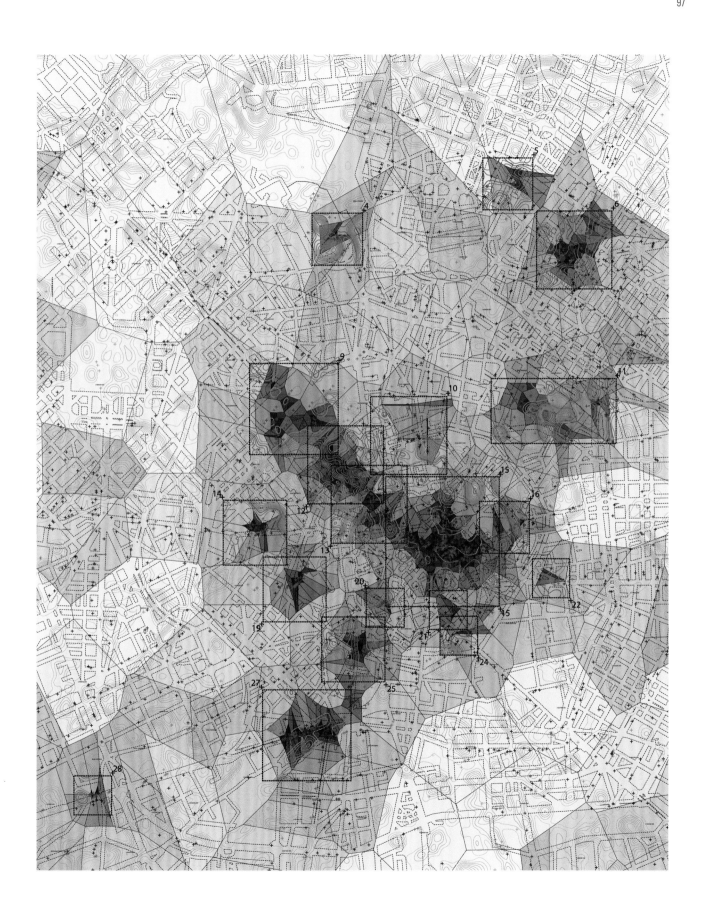

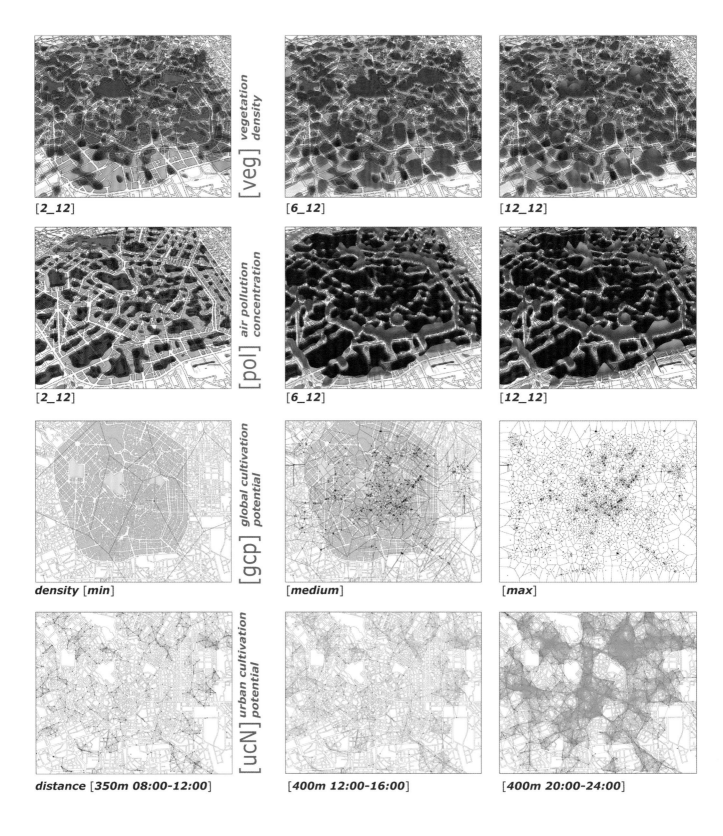

[veg] *vegetation density*

[*2_12*]  [*6_12*]  [*12_12*]

[pol] *air pollution concentration*

[*2_12*]  [*6_12*]  [*12_12*]

[gcp] *global cultivation potential*

**density** [**min**]  [**medium**]  [**max**]

[ucN] *urban cultivation potential*

**distance** [**350m 08:00-12:00**]  [**400m 12:00-16:00**]  [**400m 20:00-24:00**]

of the city that affords the indexing of multiple and non-homogeneous urban parameters for the redefinition of urban zones. Operational field maps are generated by algorithmic design logics that simulate and visualize opportunities not registered by typical urban master plans.

## The Metropolitan Proto-Garden

Driven by this vision, in 2010 we proposed the notion of cyber-gardening the city, which we tested in a series of workshops in Milan and in an interface/simulation project called the Metropolitan Proto-Garden.[3] In an attempt to contribute to the discussion initiated by the master plan for Expo 2015 (proposed by the advisory team of Stefano Boeri, Richard Burdett, Jacques Herzog, Joan Busquets, and William McDonough), we engaged with the idea of a diffuse Expo, capable of reactivating and re-metabolizing Milan's network of farms and its historically productive infrastructure.[4]

We immediately challenged the dominant eco-ideology by suggesting the introduction of a combined infrastructure of digital, real-time satellite maps of the city's new operational fields and of materially active biotechnological architectures. Presented in the form of an open-source interface, the project would augment the existing urban landscape with real-time simulations of the potential emergence of distributed and collective networks of biotechnological urban agriculture. The interface would simulate, visualize, and operate latent bio-digital mechanisms in real-time; for example, the relationship between air pollution and the uncontrolled proliferation of microalgae colonies that currently grow in the waterways of the city would be described and exploited to promote urban enhanced photosynthesis, urban oxygenation, and biomass production for both food and fuel. Augmented by biotechnological innovation, such mechanisms can feed on urban byproducts, thereby activating new pollution-to-food feedback loops, significantly affecting the overall urban metabolism, and reducing its footprint. The role of simulation here is to drastically affect the urban metabolism by increasing the interconnected flow of urban matter (e.g., algae), information (environmental sensors, social networking, and cultivation), and energy (biomass, food). Just as the discovery of oil triggered the exceptional acceleration of our societal metabolism that we call industrialization, so the implementation of urban bio-digital simulations and related biotechnological prototypes could be the key to a new industrial revolution, achieving a robust and sustainable Urbansphere.

Another ambition of our proposal was to enable a spontaneous and viral proliferation of new urban practices of bio-digital cultivation, contributing in novel and unexpected ways to an increase in the city's productivity (thus the term 'cyber-gardening'). We named our proposal a Metropolitan Proto-Garden, an urban, human-made, living and bio-digital infrastructure that would transform the city into a large terrain for collective cultivation. In this vision, urbanity augments nature rather than being in antithesis to it. The urban habitat, we contended, offers more evolved environments of communication, interaction, and cultivation of non-human living systems than the wild one does.

To test this hypothesis, we designed and built the Urban Algae Folly in the Future Food District at Expo Milano 2015. This structure attempted a radical reinterpretation of the relationship among the public realm, architecture, and the problem of feeding a booming global population. If the Proto-Garden tests the digital interface of this new urban algorithm, the Folly demonstrates its material embodiment in an architectural system, a spatial articulation of sensing devices, processing units, structural components, mechanical machines, and biological organisms.

Six years in the making, the Folly is the world's first bio-digital architecture made of a soft ethylene tetrafluoroethylene (ETFE) skin and hosting living cultures of Spirulina and Chlorella. The concept for this project emerged as we were developing the large-scale operational field maps of the Metropolitan Proto-Garden and visiting Milan's aforementioned canals and irrigation networks. In our research, we discovered a rich variety of water plants growing spontaneously, including various algae species whose properties surprised us. We discovered that their ability to photosynthesize is 10 times greater than that of large trees and that they can produce vegetable proteins with far greater efficiency than any form of animal farming. We began to realize how algal species constitute exceptionally efficient urban mechanisms, which are currently excluded from the spectrum of codified urban landscapes precisely because of the blinding effect of the dominant eco-conservative ideology.

We therefore built a digitally augmented habitat to cultivate these microorganisms as part of the expanded vision of inhabited public space contained in the Proto-Garden simulation. In this habitat, the productive capabilities of microalgae

are actually expanded by multiple levels of interference and interaction with other human and non-human systems. The innovative architecture of the Urban Algae Folly originates from the evolution of the ETFE architectural skin system. In this instance, it has the ability to provide the ideal habitat both to stimulate Spirulina's growth and to guarantee visitors' comfort. On sunny summer days, the microalgae grow rapidly, thus increasing the shading potential of the architectural skin and improving human comfort. Visitors, by their presence, activate the digital regulation system, which stimulates algal oxygenation, solar insolation, and growth. At any given moment the effective translucency, color, reflectivity, sound, and productivity of the Urban Algae Folly are the result of the symbiotic relationship of climate, microalgae, humans, and digital control systems. Data streams of temperature, pH, humidity, and human proximity and activity are fed in real time to the digital 'brain' that adjusts the algae flow. Simulated predictions of $CO_2$ adsorption, $O_2$ production, and nutrient harvesting are computed and alter the relative local operational field; local changes trigger chain reactions that in turn affect the overall urban field. These abstract, mediated, and transcalar bio-digital processes lie at the core of our new understanding of the nature of nature, which extends beyond human perception and biological constraints.

Whoever cares about sustainable urban development and an eco-systemic evolution of architectural design must love and embrace urbanity and all of its dirty and messy sides; moreover, he or she should attempt to further remove urbanity from its picturesque and pseudo-rural dimension by abstracting its material, informational, and energetic processes at a level where they are free to engender new mechanisms of transformation of the urban metabolism. We call this abstract bio-digital dimension the Urbansphere, and simulation is the tool for its synthesis. Simulation here is not understood analytically as the mere processing of data in cyberspace, but as an actual engine of synthesis; simulation does not simply predict possible futures, but contributes to their actualization in urban space and in real time.

1 In Italy, Milan is the municipality with the largest agricultural surface area after Rome, accordingly to ISTAT data from 2012. See the Open Data website of the Comune di Milano, Dati.comune.milano.it [accessed January 14, 2016]. The metropolitan area of Milan has a highly developed agricultural territory; more than half of its surface area is agricultural land or forestry land. Parco Sud is Europe's largest agricultural park and contains more than one thousand operational agricultural businesses. See Valentina Cattivelli, Eupolis Lombardia & Politecnico di Milano, "L'esperienza degli orti urbani nel comune di Milano: una lettura attraverso gli open data comunali," *Agriregionieuropa anno* 10, no. 39 [2014].

2 Jacques Herzog laments the failures of EXPO Milano to embody the core conceptual propositions of his Masterplan. His critique focuses predominantly on formal questions. See Uncube "Putting an End to the Vanity Fair," http://www.uncubemagazine.com/sixcms/detail.php?id=15358283&articleid=art-1425303037595-e330263a-ce42-485c-b9ea-acd0290cdbf2#!/page53 [accessed January 14, 2016]. Both EXPO Milano 2015 and the entire Parco Sud have perhaps more critically missed the radical technological and infrastructural opportunities that the original masterplan highlighted, which was a "weak and diffuse" agro-infrastructure to feed the bio-Milan of the future. An article that more directly highlights some of the shortcomings of the EXPO approach can be found by author Oliver Wainwright, The Guardian, "Expo 2015: what does Milan gain by hosting this bloated global extravaganza?" http://www.theguardian.com/cities/2015/may/12/expo-2015-what-does-milan-gain-by-hosting-this-bloated-global-extravaganza [accessed January 14, 2016].

3 For a more detailed description of the Metropolitan Proto-Garden project, refer to Marco Poletto & Claudia Pasquero, *Systemic Architecture* [Routledge, 2012], 238–59.

4 For the original design of the Expo 2015 Master plan, see http://www.abitare.it/en/architecture/2009/09/10/expo-2/ and http://www.designboom.com/architecture/jacques-herzog-ricky-burdett-stefano-boeri-william-mcdonough-milan-expo-2015-conceptual-masterplan/ [accessed January 14, 2016].

Previous page: Metropolitan Proto-Garden. A catalogue of Operational Fields simulated over time; fields include vegetation density, air pollution concentration, global cultivation potential, and urban cultivation potential.

Opposite: Urban Algae Folly for Braga. Close up view of the folly and its systems.

# KEEP IT

## ORON CATTS + IONAT ZURR

Oron Catts + Ionat Zurr, award winning artists, researchers, and curators, formed the internationally renowned Tissue Culture and Art Project, which explores the use of tissue technologies for cultural expressions. Catts is the Co-Founder and Director of SymbioticA: the Centre of Excellence in Biological Arts at the University of Western Australia and a Professor of Contestable Design at the Royal College for the Arts, UK. Zurr is a researcher and SymbioticA's academic coordinator. Both are Visiting Professors at Biofilia – Base for Biological Arts at Aalto University, Finland. They are considered pioneers in the field of biological art and publish and exhibit widely. Their ideas and projects reach beyond the confines of art; their work is often cited as inspiration to diverse areas such as new materials, textiles, design, architecture, ethics, fiction, and food.

✚ BIOETHICS, FOOD SCIENCE, INDUSTRIAL DESIGN

It can be argued that contemporary biology is increasingly becoming a discipline of isolation and control, particularly in the area now known as synthetic biology. Much of the rhetoric and practice in this field seems to focus on controlling living systems at the molecular level. In this paper, however, we argue that one of the fundamental vehicles of controlling life–something that engineering biology can't do without, and something that closely links biology and architecture in its many manifestations–is the ability to simulate and control the environmental conditions of the biological body. Here we will explore this argument through the story of the incubator, a simulator of bodies and a homeostatic surrogate for life out of context, out of place, and out of agency.

Life evolves through the interplay of existing traits and their adaptation to changing environmental conditions. Many organisms opt to keep their insides shielded in near-optimal conditions in order to maintain their biological functioning and homeostatic equilibrium. Human technology enables artificial environments to preserve life outside its proper context, in situations where it would otherwise die. In other words, humans have developed artificial 'bodies' to support life out of context – on land, under water, and even in space. Some life or parts of life–fragments of bodies such as cells, tissues, and other lab-grown life–depend on carefully controlled, artificially simulated conditions. Without constant technological support from 'providers' like the incubator, these forms of de-contextualized life will die.

Generally, incubators are taken for granted in the biotech world while other technological control systems, such as molecular interventions, take center stage. The same attitude rules in the hyperbolic discourse of synthetic biology. Here we would like to emphasize the importance and the associated problems of simulated environmental conditions, not only in maintaining life but also in shaping it, in both the biological and the cultural sense. We argue that replacing the grounding of life in a code (i.e., DNA) with a context- or environment-dependent basis constitutes more than a scientific issue; it is an ideologically charged view of life.

Opposte: *Victimless Leather- A Prototype of Stitch-less Jacket grown in a Technoscientific "Body"* by The Tissue Culture and Art Project (Oron Catts & Ionat Zurr).

WARM!

INCUBATORS AS SIMULATORS

However, let us go back for now to the inconspicuous, rarely mentioned Incubator, a simulator of bodies, which plays a significant role in the life of cells and other forms of de-contextualized life. An incubator can be described as an isolated environment that controls heat, humidity and, in some cases, additional elements such as gas content, pH level, and other mechanical conditions. It is a homeostatic, dynamic, surrogate body that shields fragile life from the external environment.

One of the first recorded methods of incubating involved using heat from rotting and burning manure to warm chicken eggs: "At around 3,000 years ago, the early Egyptian incubators consisted of a large mud brick building with a series of small rooms [ovens] located at each side of a central passageway. In the upper part of these 'small incubation rooms,' there were shelves for burning straw, camel manure or charcoal in order to provide radiant heat to the eggs below."[1] Mechanical incubating, known as the 'artificial mother,' was invented in 1747 by René Reamur in Paris, France.[2] The first commercial incubator was developed by Charles Hearson in 1881.[3] These early inventions enabled eggs to mature without the need for a chicken, and they also enabled a year-round supply of chickens. Through the ability to simulate the hen's brooding functions, chickens and eggs became an industrial commodity, engineered by human technology.

The later development of the human incubator is intriguing, not so much as a technological advancement—as it followed the same principles as chicken incubators—but rather because of how it was perceived, understood, and presented to society. Incubator aesthetics [even if materially transparent] and the design of the 'packaging' in which the abstracted womb simulator resided, as we will see, had much to do with capturing the public imagination and played a major role in the articulation of the real life inside the machine.

Although the invention of incubators for premature infants was associated with the French obstetrician Stéphane Tarnier, it was Dr Martin A. Couney, a European physician, who introduced this idea to the United States in a rather unorthodox way: through fairgrounds.[4] Dr Couney brought his incubator 'show' to the Pan-American Exposition in Buffalo in 1901: "As with other attractions at a fair, a 'barker' tried to entice people into the 'premie' exhibit located in a 'neat and artistic' brick building."[5] This exhibit took its place among the other entertainments along the Exposition midway, which included an Eskimo village, "Beautiful Orient," and "Trip to the Moon." When the exposition closed due to political and economic upheavals, Couney moved the show to a permanent position at Coney Island in Brooklyn, New York, where it was one of the first permanent displays. This exhibit, complete with living infants, remained there from 1903 to 1941. As one source reported:

> [V]isitors to Couney's exhibit could [after purchasing a ticket and walking through the audience designated aisles] watch nasal feeding through a glass window; doubtless, the spectacle captured their imaginations as a simultaneously advanced and freakish alimentary display. Breast-feeding, a process central to maternity, delivered itself to mechanical production and an aesthetic display.[6]

Couney's incubators were designed beyond their functional needs as a spectacle for public view. At the same time, the incubator was not a transparent environment with regard to the life it carried; rather, it played an active and dynamic role in the biological and cultural articulation of premature human babies. Due to the nature of its role as a simulator, the incubator was not only instrumental in the transition of these liminal beings toward a healthy life but also provided scientific and cultural classifications. The simulation was initially articulated via aesthetic rather than scientific modes of presentation, as a device that enabled

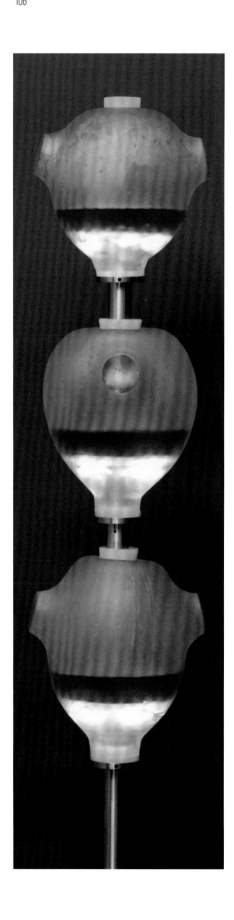

the infant to progress from an ambiguous 'passage zone' to personhood, at which point it could assume its own political life outside the incubator once it had matured sufficiently. In the meantime, while housed in this passage zone hosted by an artificial mother, the premature baby became a 'thing,' a freak, a 'semi-being' (neither human nor animal) – an object/subject that could be put on display as a curiosity until it could be 'normalized' and 'approved' by the techno-scientific project and become assimilated into the classification of life as a human being. Moreover, this marriage of bodies and technologies via a simulated mother–where life exists (at least temporarily) only within a techno-scientific body–has opened the door to many other applications, both imaginary and real.[7]

This brief history of the incubator provides the context for introducing some nonhuman applications with their own set of consequences. Shortly after the introduction of human incubators, scientists developed ways to culture tissue cells, isolated from the complex body. These cells could grow and proliferate within a technological support system that simulated particular aspects of the body's environment; they were thus incubators in the more contemporary language of 'bioreactors.'[8] They were also a rarely acknowledged type of cybernetic organism that combined a biological body with artificial life support.

A rough estimate would put the current biomass of living cells and tissues disassociated from the bodies that once hosted them, in the thousands of tons. In addition, there exist many tons of fragments of bodies (cells, tissues, organs) maintained in suspended animation in cryogenic conditions, all of which require intensive technological intervention (in other words, technological simulation of biological processes) to prevent their transformation into a non-living state. Much of this living biological matter can, in theory, be co-cultured and fused (cell fusion), or joined together within sterile environments (with varying degrees of success). Age, gender, race, species, and location do not play the same roles in the simulated body as with other living bodies. This means that, in theory, every tissue in every living being has the potential to become part of a collection of living fragments that will be brought together at some future point within the context and with the support of the simulated body. With the introduction of simulated bodies, the biological entities existing within them have been rendered almost invisible. These types of being (or semi-being or semi-living) do not fall within current biological or even cultural classifications.[9] Furthermore, the environments sustaining these cells exist but are usually rendered as neutral or transparent.

This aesthetic of invisibility may serve to make the cells and tissues devoid of agency, extracted and abstracted from the body from which they were derived as well as from the 'body' they have become. In addition, it renders the technology invisible and therefore neutral or even natural

**1** Marcelo Paniago, "Artificial Incubation of Poultry Eggs: 3,000 Years of History," *Hatchery Expertise Online* (September 2005), http://www.thepoultrysite.com/focus/contents/ceva/OnlineBulletins/ob_2005/Article-No2-Sept05.pdf (accessed December 3, 2015).

**2** Sigfried Giedion, *Mechanisation Takes Command: A Contribution to Anonymous History* (New York: Oxford University Press, 1948), 248.

**3** C.E. Hearson, "Apparatus for Heating Eggs by Artificial Heat," No. 298,579. Patented May 13, 1884. Cited in https://www.google.com/patents/US298579 (accessed December 9, 2015).

**4** A visit to the chicken incubator display in the Paris zoo inspired Tarnier to have the zoo's instrument maker install a similar device for the care of infants in 1880.

**5** University at Buffalo Libraries, "Baby Incubator Exhibit at the Pan-American Exposition in Buffalo," http://library.buffalo.edu/pan-am/exposition/health/medical/incubators.html (accessed December 3, 2015).

**6** Scott Webel, "Kinderbrutanstalt: Leisure space and the Coney Island baby incubators," *Text, Practice, Performance* V (2003): 9.

**7** The 'simulated mother' idea led J.B.S. Haldane to predict in 1924 that by 2074, or 150 years later, 70% of all human births will result from pregnancies nurtured in an artificial environment from fertilization to birth. He called it ectogenesis, and this notion of the nonhuman taking over the most fundamental aspects of becoming a biological human became material for *Brave New World*'s totalitarian nightmares and for transhumanist dreams. Haldane's prediction may yet be proved right, although it currently seems that ectogenesis is at least a generation away, but in the meantime a new form of bio-labor, the surrogate biological mother, has considerably blurred the line between simulated and real motherhood.

(like 'Mother Earth'), as if the technology itself were leaving no footprint on the environment but serving simply as an autotrophic artificial mother.

To illustrate how the incubator's role has become completely ignored or transparent, consider the marketing of in-vitro meat technology. In-vitro meat is an attempt to grow meat using tissue culture and tissue engineering techniques without directly killing animals. In this case, a simulated technological body is replacing the animal body, and only the tissue of interest is grown for its eventual human consumption. We were among the first to grow and eat in-vitro meat (in 2000 and 2003, respectively) and have written extensively about the issues surrounding this development.[10] We see a considerable disconnect between the actual biological issues involved and the fantasies that seem prevalent in much of the discourse around in-vitro meat. We argue that in-vitro meat is a symptom of the problems inherent in the artificial simulation of 'bodies,' as it presents the isolation and control of life as an ethical alternative to meat consumption rather than as a semi-permeable contextualization of living matter within an environment. In addition, in-vitro meat alludes to the urbanization of food production from the field to the lab and the factory, as demonstrated by the names of the two main companies driving its commercialization: Modern Meadow and New Harvest.

In much of the media coverage of the development of in-vitro meat, the laboratory, which stands for the simulated artificial environment that has replaced both the field and the animal body, is seen as a black box of control and growth in which meat is magically produced, as if out of thin air. The actual resources needed in order to grow cells into a piece of meat are usually downplayed or totally ignored. Instead, the opaque and physical, albeit technologically simulated, body is transformed into a virtual and transparent 'body' that requires no input. This attitude can be traced to one of the most cited papers used to advocate in-vitro meat as a more environmentally friendly mode of meat production.

Previous page: Infant Incubators, Pan-American Exhibition, Buffalo, NY, (1901).

Opposite: *Triptych of Dismembered Immortality 2015* by Oron Catts, Robert Foster (Fink Design).

Titled "Environmental Impacts of Cultured Meat Production," this paper, commissioned by New Harvest, is an exercise in agenda-driven theoretical simulation that uses some outrageous assumptions and explanations to describe a product that does not yet exist.[11] With regard to the incubator, which provides a constant, stable, warm environment with the right combination of gases and is one of the most important requirements for cell growth, the paper makes this curious statement: "As cells produce heat during the growth, additional energy inputs in heating of the reactor are not required."[12]

In addition to the fact that it is impossible to incubate cells purely by their self-generated heat (at the beginning of the growth cycle there could not be enough cells to produce such heat), we find quite interesting here the negation of the incubator's role as an active 'agent' that must be responsive to signals from the living elements grown within it. In short, an incubator does not provide virtual, transparent simulation of the body in growing life, but is an actual, active simulator of real conditions that require constant input and output of activity and energy. Even though the physical incubator is a simulation of a biological body, it still needs to mediate between this internal ambient environment and the real world.

Let us take the concept of the simulator as artificial mother to a larger scale. The notion of a building as insulated life support is continually played out in current discourses on sustainability in architecture, wherein buildings are conceptualized as hermetic containers with narrow system boundaries.[13] Structures are envisioned as incubators or bioreactors that isolate and simulate a controlled environment with supposedly optimum conditions (and hence as separate from the harsh, toxic environment around them). This rhetoric of sustainability is frequently heard in connection to the development of smart buildings, which use multiple sensing technologies to maintain the homeostatic conditions of the healthy house/bioreactor.

Going beyond the question of whether the use of energy to simulate artificial environmental conditions is sustainable, a more fundamental question must be asked: can such a simulation replace the 'real' environment or even improve on it, especially in a future scenario in which our planetary environment becomes uninhabitable for human life?

Some clues to the problems associated with this form of simulation appear in research by people who study buildings and their mechanical systems. Buildings that are not open to the external environment, even if ventilated, tend to create harmful air microbiomes rather than healthy ones.[14] In other words, buildings that attempt to keep the outdoors out are actually the least healthy for us. Isolated buildings with mechanical ventilation–air simulators rather than air conditioners–can result in biomes that will eventually be harmful to the other forms of life residing there. The main problem with simulated environments that must be kept insulated (as opposed to the body's semi-permeable characteristics) is that the decontextualized life becomes isolated and sustains a monoculture, in both the physical and conceptual sense.

Buildings need to be less like incubators and more like bodies, not merely simulators of so-called ideal, but actually misguided conditions. This is particularly important to consider as we face intensified climate volatility and an escalating demand for the design and engineering of isolated self-sufficient 'biopods' to protect increasingly decontextualized forms of life from the harsh external environment. The aesthetics and rhetoric associated with such idealized human technological environments that have the ability to isolate and control may in the end be harmful and threatening rather than providers of salvation and comfort. The impossibility of total control through technology may, after all, help to preserve the importance of leakage, contamination, diversity, and fertilization as keys to survival. The Artificial Mother as a replacement for Mother Earth may be a patriarchal fantasy, but, as the prospect of geoengineering the planet's ecosystems becomes more likely, earth might become indistinguishable from a simulated life support system.

**8** As Eduard Uhlenhuth explained in 1916: "Through the discovery of tissue culture we have, so to speak, created a new type of body on which to grow the cell." Uhlenhuth, "Changes in Pigment Epithelium Cells and Iris Pigment Cells of Rana Pipiens Induced by Changes in Environmental Conditions," *Journal of Experimental Medicine* 24 (1916): 690.

**9** For more details, see Oron Catts & Ionat Zurr, "The Biopolitics of Life Removed from Context: Neolifism," in S.E. Wilmer & Audronė Žukauskaitė (eds) *Resisting Biopolitics: Philosophical, Political, and Performative Strategies* (New York: Routledge, 2015), 135–58.

**10** Oron Catts & Ionat Zurr, "Growing for Different Ends," *International Journal of Biochemistry & Cell Biology*, Vol. 56 (2014): 20–9.; Ionat Zurr & Oron Catts, "Disembodied Livestock: The Promise of a Semi-Living Utopia," *Parallex* 66 (2013).

**11** Hanna L. Tuomisto & M. Joost Teixeira de Mattos, "Environmental Impacts of Cultured Meat Production," *Environmental Science and Technology* 45, no. 14 (2011): 6117–23.

**12** Ibid, 6118–19.

**13** Kiel Moe, "Iatrogenic Architecture: Unreliable Narratives of Sustainability," *Harvard Design Magazine* 40 http://www.harvarddesignmagazine.org/issues/40/iatrogenic-architecture-unreliable-narratives-of-sustainability (accessed December 3, 2015).

**14** For example, see Jessica Green's research on hospitals. She states that the "mechanical ventilation does get rid of many types of microbes, but the wrong kinds: the ones left in the hospital are much more likely to be pathogens." Healthy Heating, "Microbes: Buildings Are Complex Ecosystems," http://www.healthyheating.com/Definitions/Indoor_air_quality_definitions/Microbials-Jessica-Green-Ted-Talks.htm#.Vi2VC7crLlU (accessed December 3, 2015).

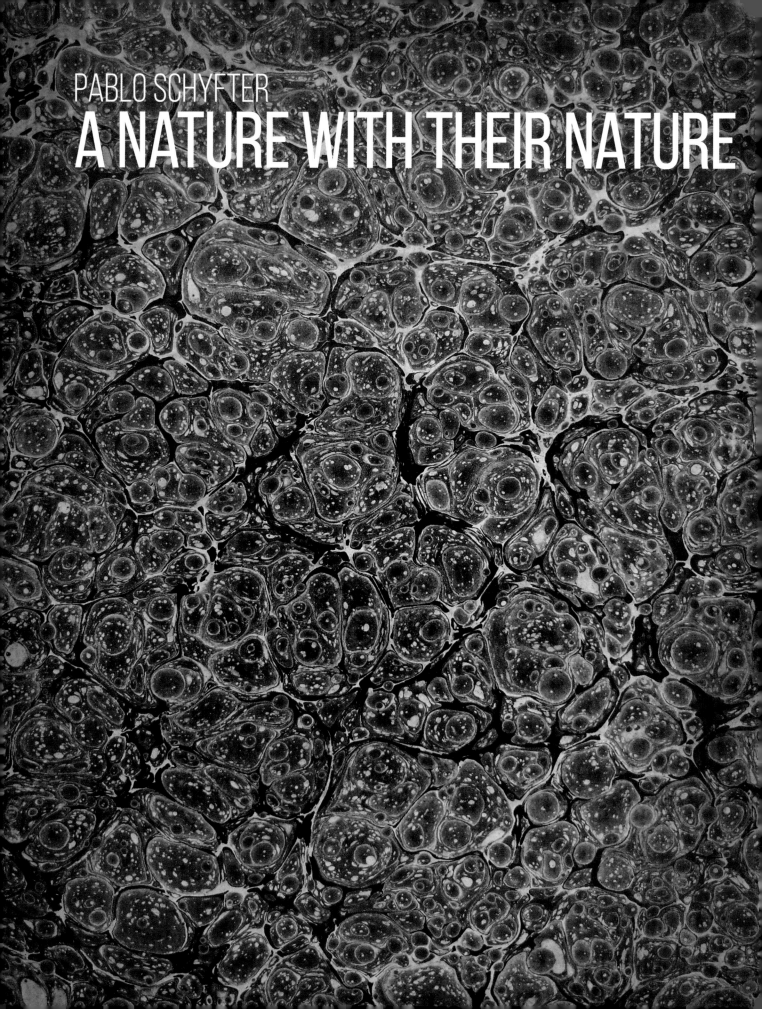

PABLO SCHYFTER

# A NATURE WITH THEIR NATURE

Pablo Schyfter works in feminist science and technology studies, and in the philosophical and sociological study of synthetic biology. In 2010 and 2011 he helped develop and carry out 'Synthetic Aesthetics,' an international project involving collaborations between artists and designers, and synthetic biologists. Currently Schyfter is lecturer in Science, Technology and Innovation Studies at the University of Edinburgh.

+ BIOCHEMISTRY, BIOETHICS, DESIGN

Synthetic biology eludes conclusive definition. As an incipient field, discipline, project, or ambition, it takes neither a singular form, nor does its membership [which is heterogeneous] practice in a synchronized manner.[1] Nonetheless, synthetic biologists have clustered into semi-distinct factions, each of which has its own particular understanding of the field and its own particular ways of practicing. Among these is a group that promises to deliver a field of 'true' or 'authentic' engineering – a field that will carry on as do existing, established disciplines of engineering, but with a living substrate.[2] The group argues that achieving this aim demands the importing and deployment of principles, ideas, and forms of work from traditional engineering.[3] These components, the synthetic biologists argue, will ensure 'true' engineering by shaping the new field using established engineering as a model.

This same group dedicates special attention and effort to one principle and practice: rational design. In laying out his vision for synthetic biology, Drew Endy proposes to replace the existing "expensive, unreliable and *ad hoc* research process" with what Tom Knight describes as "the intentional design, modeling, construction, debugging, and testing of artificial living systems."[4] Put simply, these researchers and others hope to make planning and building with living stuff as systematic and standardized as building with things like electronic circuitry. Rational design in synthetic biology hinges in part on simulations of living nature as technological artifice. These simulations in turn rely on representations of biology as something that carries an inherent potential for rational design.

In 2010 and 2011, an interdisciplinary, innovative project entitled "Synthetic Aesthetics" paired synthetic biologists with artists and designers in collaborative projects aimed at exploring just what design entails in synthetic biology.[5] Each pair was given funds to support spending an equal amount of time in the lab and in the studio, along with freedom to explore design as they saw fit. One of these teams–synthetic biologist Fernan Federici and architect David Benjamin–placed rational design and digital simulation at the crux of their work. As already noted, rational design is central to the engineering faction of synthetic biology; digital simulation is one tool that these practitioners have proposed to assist their design work.[6] The results of Federici and Benjamin's project offer a useful perspective from which to examine many important aspects of synthetic biology's pursuit of rational design. Federici and Benjamin's digital simulations of plant cell growth rested on a collection of representations akin to many of those frequently used in synthetic biology. Most importantly, these representations all involve casting living things as entities carrying design potential. For Federici and Benjamin, plant cells were conceived as logical problem solvers; for synthetic biology, all manner of biological stuff is rationally designable material. In both cases, the practitioners do not capture a singular and freestanding 'nature of nature' but instead deliver a nature consistent with *their* nature.

## From cells to buildings

Federici and Benjamin's collaboration made use of their shared interests and combined abilities. In broad terms, the pair studied the self-organizing dynamics of xylem cells using biological imaging tools and architectural computer simulations. Xylem cells form a part of plants' vascular system. The cells are curious due to their capacity to develop a form of exoskeleton, a structure that helps to give shape to the organism's vascular system. Federici and Benjamin set out to study the self-organizing abilities of xylem cells by simulating how the cells construct their exoskeletons in specific spatial conditions. Studying this phenomenon served a broader and bolder aim – capturing the cells' biological 'logic.'

Federici and Benjamin posited the notion of biological 'logic' as the driving mechanism underlying xylem cells' capacity to build. 'Logic' here refers to the problem-solving capability inherent in these plant cells. The two researchers believe that using imaging tools and computer simulations to identify and capture this 'logic' can serve both synthetic biology and architecture. The former may gain a tool for analyzing how biology organizes; the latter may find novel ways to engage with and harness the living world. For the architect, biological 'logic' might provide techniques for resolving structural problems in innovative and unexpectedly curious ways, and it could enlist biology as an aid to architecture as more than a reserve of forms to mimic.

To study how xylem cells self-organize and build their structures, Federici and Benjamin introduced artificial walls and boundaries into a colony of the cells, and they then tracked how the cells built their structures within the constrained spaces. In other words, they posed a structural quandary and watched as the xylem cells produced a solution, hoping that simulating the process digitally would reveal the 'logic' underlying the cells' growth. As the cells developed, they were photographed using confocal microscopy. The images of the exoskeletons were then transformed into a point-vector computer model and the growing process was quantified into a body of numerical data. Finally, the pair used Eureqa, a software tool, to develop equations approximating relationships between the data. Federici and Benjamin argued that these equations capture the cells' biological 'logic' in mathematical form.

The team's next experiment involved more direct engagement with architecture and architectural simulations. Federici and Benjamin again created a model based on photographs of the cells. However, rather than quantifying growth and deriving equations, the two treated the model as one of a human-scale structure (such as a building). They explain:

> We applied architectural scale, materials, and loading conditions to the 3D model. Then, we supposed that our goals for the architecture-scale exoskeleton were to use the least amount of materials to achieve the least structural displacement. We ran an automated algorithm to generate, evaluate, and evolve multiple design permutations.[7]

Federici and Benjamin argue that the shape of the xylem cells' exoskeleton is one optimized for the conditions under which these cells grow—microscopic spaces and biological materials—and *not* one optimized for the scale, materials, and goals of human design and construction. However, by using architectural optimization software, the team framed xylem cells and their 'logic' as design collaborators and as a design tool, respectively. The cells offer different solutions from those typically proposed by the human architect.

## Simulations, representation and the 'out-there'

Methodologically, Federici and Benjamin's work was an exercise in simulation. The pair's models simulate cells and human structures, along with how those

Opposite: A formation of xylem cells taken from an *Arabidopsis thaliana* plant.

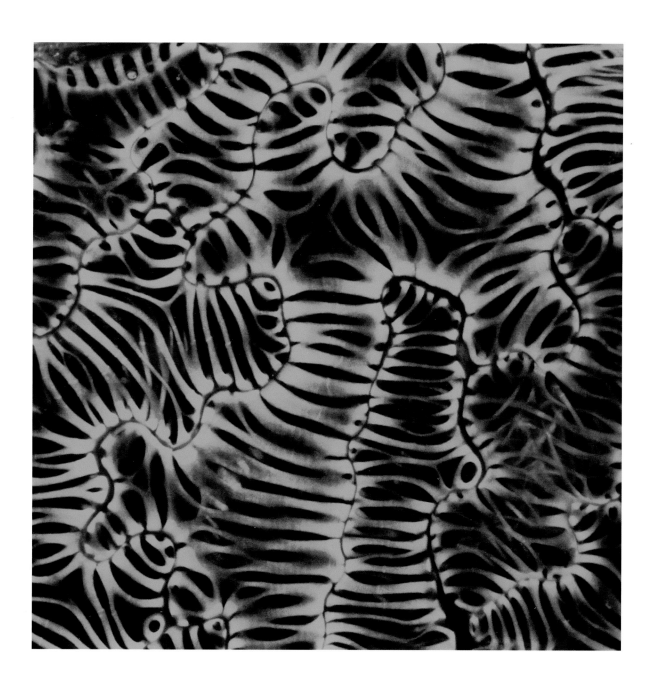

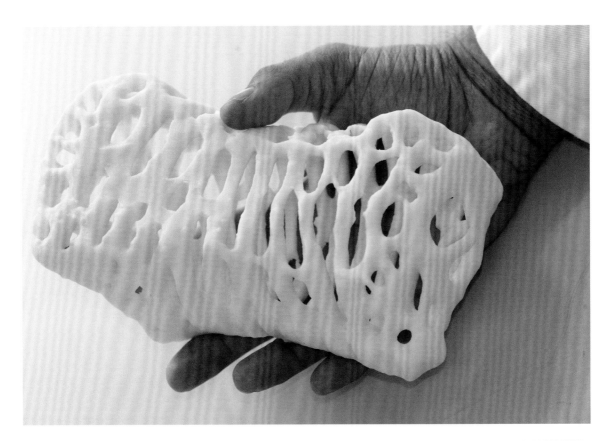

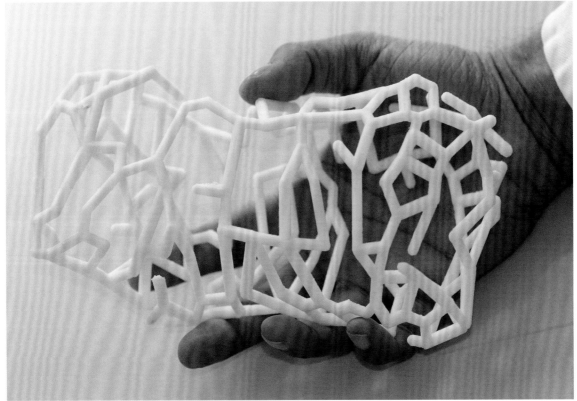

cells and structures behave in particular situations. Federici and Benjamin's simulations were of course representations. In fact, the project produced and employed many types of representations, such as photographs, models, numerical data, and equations. These representations, including the computer simulations, were deployed for the purpose of making biological logic something observable and usable. Two key underlying presuppositions drove the project, namely, the beliefs that biological 'logic' exists in itself and that it can somehow be captured – in other words, that it is out there and that we are capable of discovering it.

Commonplace understandings of representation rely on the premise that some 'out-there' must exist to be represented in the first place. Thus, simulations are facsimiles or portrayals of something independently present in the world. However, as Steve Woolgar and Michael Lynch (among others) argue, the supposition of a free-standing 'out-there' is often wrong.[8] In some instances, the idea of a self-standing entity that representations replicate or approximate fails because without representational tools, the entity cannot be witnessed at all.[9] Federici and Benjamin's xylem cells are not accessible to us without instruments like microscopy and photography. In other cases, representations are the only reality at hand. The pair's biological 'logic' does not exist in the sense in which we typically use the term; rather, it is present only by way of mathematical equations, not independent spatio-temporal being. This is also the case with synthetic biology's view of a free-standing design potential in living nature; outside this field and its pursuit of a 'true' engineering, there is no assumption of rationality or design potential in biology. Rationality is a matter theorized by synthetic biology, just as biological 'logic' is something of Federici and Benjamin's doing and is characterized by the particularities of their specific collaboration. The idiosyncrasies of the team molded both the process by which the purported biological 'logic' was made 'witnessable' and the form that the resulting representations took. Crucially, this work rested on a particular view of the living things under study – a view that in turn relies on conceptions of design. Specifically, synthetic biology's view of a rationally designable biology rests on an understanding of design that is imported from established engineering.

Federici and Benjamin's work cast the cells as logical entities engaged in rational design, and it did so by way of three interlinked depictions. First, xylem cells are problem solvers (like architects); they practice skillfully. Second, their behavior is ordered (like architectural work); their practice has procedure. Third, this order can be systematized (as is the case with architectural work); the procedure can be arranged. The three suppositions are abstractions of architectural agents, practices, and orders, respectively. Thus, in trying to 'find' the 'logic' of biology Federici and Benjamin framed the xylem cells and their growth as agents practicing a vocation that involves systematic practices.

**1** Adam Arkin, et al., "Synthetic Biology: What's in a Name?" *Nature Biotechnology* 27, no. 12 (2009).

**2** Drew Endy, "Foundations for Engineering Biology," *Nature* 438, no. 24 (2005); Endy, "Synthetic Biology: Can We Make Biology Easy to Engineer?" *Industrial Biotechnology* 4, no. 4 (2008); Susanna C. Finlay, "Engineering Biology? Exploring Rhetoric, Practice, Constraints and Collaborations within a Synthetic Biology Research Centre," *Engineering Studies* 5, no. 1 (2013).

**3** Ernesto Andrianantoandro, et al., "Synthetic Biology: New Engineering Rules for an Emerging Discipline," *Molecular Systems Biology* 2 (2006); Vincent De Lorenzo & Antoine Danchin, "Synthetic Biology: Discovering New Worlds and New Words," *EMBO Reports* 9, no. 9 (2008).

**4** Endy, "Foundations for Engineering Biology," 449; Tom Knight, "Engineering Novel Life," *Molecular Systems Biology* 1 (2005): 1.

**5** Daisy Ginsberg, et al., *Synthetic Aesthetics: Investigating Synthetic Biology's Designs on Nature* (Cambridge, MA: MIT Press, 2014).

**6** Priscilla E. M. Purnick & Ron Weiss, "The Second Wave of Synthetic Biology," *Nature Review Molecular Cell Biology* 10, no. 6 (2009).

**7** David Benjamin & Fernan Federici, "Bio-Logic," in Ginsberg, et al. *Synthetic Aesthetics*, 148.

**8** Michael Lynch, "Science in the Age of Mechanical Reproduction: Moral and Epistemic Relations between Diagrams and Photographs," *Biology & Philosophy* 6, no. 2 (1991); Steve Woolgar, "Struggles with Representation: Could It Be Otherwise?" in Catelijne Coopmans, et al. (eds) *Representation in Scientific Practice Revisited* (Cambridge, MA: MIT Press, 2014).

**9** M. Norton Wise, "Making Visible," *Isis* 97, no. 1 (2006).

**10** Adam Arkin, "Setting the Standard in Synthetic Biology," *Nature Biotechnology* 26, no. 7 (2008); Endy, "Foundations for Engineering Biology."

Opposite, top: A 3D model of a xylem cell structure.

Opposite, bottom: A 3D model of a xylem structure that has been evolved computationally using architectural software.

The three depictions support the team's search for 'out-there' biological 'logic.' For Federici and Benjamin, biological 'logic' may not exist materially as do the cells themselves, but nonetheless it is something that the cells 'have.' 'Logic' is not something *postulated*, but something captured with photography and simulation. Crucially, the pair's concept of 'logic' exists as one part of an overarching depiction of xylem cells as living things engaged in systematic practices. Federici and Benjamin rendered the cells 'logical' by treating them as logical entities.

## The potential for rational design

Federici and Benjamin examined and simulated this biological 'logic' by exploring instrumental links between architecture and synthetic biology and by approaching xylem cells as if they are structural problem solvers. Making the cells' 'logic' into something witnessable and functional for epistemic and design practices was a project particular to the pair. The objects under study and the things being produced were *by* and *of* the pair, and they reflected the idiosyncrasies of the collaboration. Synthetic biology presents a similar case.

Representations in synthetic biology seek to draw out what the discipline views as an inherent potential for rational design. As I noted above, one of synthetic biology's most vocal factions champions a view of the field as 'true' or 'authentic' engineering. Synthetic biologists in general promise to deliver innovative technologies using the stuff of living nature, and many argue that such technologies will have positive economic and environmental ramifications. Those who aim at engineering authenticity supplement these promises with visions of particular forms of design and fabrication. Authenticity, they argue, will follow from importing and employing so-called 'engineering principles' such as standardization of parts, decoupling of processes, design-build-test cycles, and rational design.[10] Practitioners hope that such principles can structure engineering work with a biological substrate, just as effectively as the same principles have structured civil engineering work with metal and concrete.

In its work with engineering principles, synthetic biology relies greatly on representations of living things as objects *of* and *for* engineering. Segments of DNA are discussed as discrete 'parts.' When such parts are linked functionally, they become 'devices.' When devices are combined, the result is a 'system.' Systems can then be inserted into a supporting cell, or a 'chassis.' Experimenters comprehend, design, and build their biological artifacts using analogies, many of which are taken from electronics. Practitioners often represent genetic constructs as circuits of logic gates; a string of nucleotides becomes an AND gate, another an OR gate.[11] Such depictions cast the relationships and behaviors of living stuff in the mold of human artifice.

Laboratory work based on these representations has delivered biological equivalents of electronic devices like oscillators, switches, and counters.[12] This work and its depictions of living nature are bound by an essential commitment: if synthetic biologists are to design rationally, as do those in established engineering professions, the material which they employ must be *rationally designable*. Researchers argue that "general 'design principles'–profoundly shaped by the constraints of evolution–govern the structure and function of [biological] modules."[13] Both the modular organization of living things and the rational, designable character of such parts are found in living things themselves. As such, one mission of synthetic biology is "uncovering biological design principles."[14] Doing so is congruous with the field's ambition to carry out 'authentic' engineering with a living substrate, since "a number of the design principles of biological systems are familiar to engineers."[15] A 2011 publication on techniques and constructs that support "digital-like synthetic biology" states that just as "Boolean logic gates are widely used in electronic circuits to build digital devices, logic operations are encoded in gene regulatory networks that cells use to cascade and integrate multiple environmental and cellular signals and to respond accordingly."[16] The authors do not simply employ an analogy to electronic systems based on Boolean logic. Like other synthetic biologists, they argue that the dynamics underlying electronic circuitry are already present in the biology itself, housed in "biological control modules"[17] that can be exploited and re-engineered. That is, rational behavior–and consequently the potential for rational design and re-design–is a quality of the biology itself.

Federici and Benjamin rendered 'logic' as something inherent in xylem cells, usable by people but ultimately free-standing. Synthetic biology effectively does the same for rationality. This representation is indispensable to a group that aims to create a new type of engineering in the mold of prior forms of engineering. Representations of nucleotides as components that can be disconnected and reconnected in rational and functionally predictable ways serve to render a potential for rational design.[18] As with Federici and Benjamin's 'logic,' this potential is cast as an independent 'out-there.' Synthetic biology can find it, make it witnessable, and harness it to accomplish rational design with biology.

Nonetheless, the potential for rational design is no more an independently existing 'out-there' than is Federici and Benjamin's 'logic.' Synthetic biology's 'out-there' potential exists through the field's representations, and is thus something *by* and *of* that field. Casting living nature as something that carries within it a potential for rational design requires ignoring properties that do not fit the picture of synthetic biology as 'true' engineering, such as irrationality and unpredictability. Doing so allows the potential for rational design to become witnessable and usable. By portraying a capacity that can be exploited by engineering, representations of potential make the stuff of living nature something that synthetic biology can use to design and to build. Moreover, the potential becomes something that helps to authenticate the field, its ambitions, and its work.

Representations are often seen as facsimiles of something else – facsimiles that lack the original's wholeness and that often distort its free-standing truth. In both the specific case of Federici and Benjamin's project and the ongoing case of synthetic biology, representation is not an imperfect journey toward an indelible reality. Instead, representation is an attempt to render things in particular ways for particular ends.

Federici and Benjamin simulated xylem cells as things enrolled for architecture, as instruments for and partners in design. The pair's biological 'logic' is *their* 'logic,' and outside their partnership it does not exist. The entities that Federici and Benjamin studied possess a 'logic' because they were situated in a particular partnership. The living things of synthetic biology carry design potential because they are situated in a particular field with specific ambitions. The field's rational design potential is similarly *its own* vision – a capacity to plan and build with biology and situate synthetic biology in the tradition of engineering.

Representations of biology as mechanical or electronic are not false depictions that are detrimental to some pursuit of truth, but consciously selected portrayals that satisfy a vision of rational design and construction. Synthetic biologists are working to create an identity for 'authentic engineering' that they can enlist as useful for their field. Casting living things as entities that carry a potential for rational design serves that mission. As such, these researchers are not working to capture the single, conclusive 'nature of nature.' Rather, they are seeking to deliver a nature consistent with *their* nature – *living stuff of engineering and for engineering*.

11 Harvey Lederman, et al., "Deoxyribozyme-Based Three-Input Logic Gates and Construction of a Molecular Full Adder," *Biochemistry* 45, no. 4 (2006); Keller Rinaudo, et al., "A Universal RNAi-Based Logic Evaluator That Operates in Mammalian Cells," *Nature Biotechnology* 25, no. 7 (2007); Jerome Bonnet, et al., "Amplifying Genetic Logic Gates," *Science* 340, no. 6132 (2013).

12 On oscillators, see Michael B. Elowitz & Stanislas Leibler, "A Synthetic Oscillatory Network of Transcriptional Regulators," *Nature* 403, no. 6765 (2000); David McMillen, et al., "Synchronizing Genetic Relaxation Oscillators by Intercell Signalling," *Proceedings of the National Academies of Science* 99, no. 2 (2002); Jesse Stricker, et al., "A Fast, Robust and Tunable Synthetic Gene Oscillator," *Nature* 456, no. 7203 (2008). On switches, see Timothy S. Gardner, Charles R. Cantor, & James J. Collins, "Construction of a Genetic Toggle Switch in *Escherichia coli*," *Nature* 403, no. 6767 (2000); Mariette R. Atkinson, et al., "Development of Genetic Circuitry Exhibiting Toggle Switch or Oscillatory Behavior in *Escherichia coli*," *Cell* 113, no. 5 (2003); Azi Lipshtat, et al., "Genetic Toggle Switch without Cooperative Binding," *Physical Review Letters* 96, 188101 (2006). On counters, see Ari. E. Friedland, et al., "Synthetic Gene Networks That Count," *Science* 324, no. 5931 (2009).

13 Leland H. Hartwell, et al., "From Molecular to Modular Cell Biology," *Nature* 402, no. 6761 supp. (1999): 47.

14 Ibid., 51.

15 Ibid., 50.

16 Baojung Wang, et al., "Engineering Modular and Orthogonal Genetic Logic Gates for Robust Digital-Like Synthetic Biology," *Nature Communications* 2 (2011), doi:10.1038/ncomms1516.

17 Ibid.

18 Steve Benner & Michael Sismour, "Synthetic Biology," *Nature Reviews Genetics* 6 (2005), doi:10.1038/nrg1637.

# IMAGE CREDITS

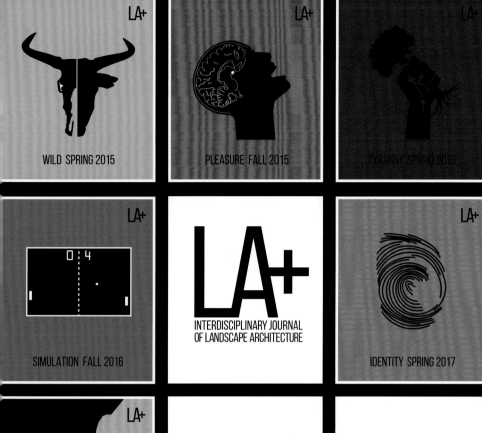

WILD  SPRING 2015

PLEASURE  FALL 2015

TYRANNY  SPRING 2016

SIMULATION  FALL 2016

# LA+

## INTERDISCIPLINARY JOURNAL
## OF LANDSCAPE ARCHITECTURE

IDENTITY  SPRING 2017

RISK  FALL 2017

# UPCOMING ISSUES

LA+ (Landscape Architecture Plus) from the University of Pennsylvania School of Design is the first truly interdisciplinary journal of landscape architecture. Within its pages you will hear not only from designers, but also from historians, artists, philosophers, psychologists, geographers, sociologists, planners, scientists, and others. Our aim is to reveal connections and build collaborations between landscape architecture and other disciplines by exploring each issue's theme from multiple perspectives.

LA+ brings you a rich collection of contemporary thinkers and designers in two issues each year. To subscribe follow the links at WWW.LAPLUSJOURNAL.COM